THIS BOOK

belongs to

....

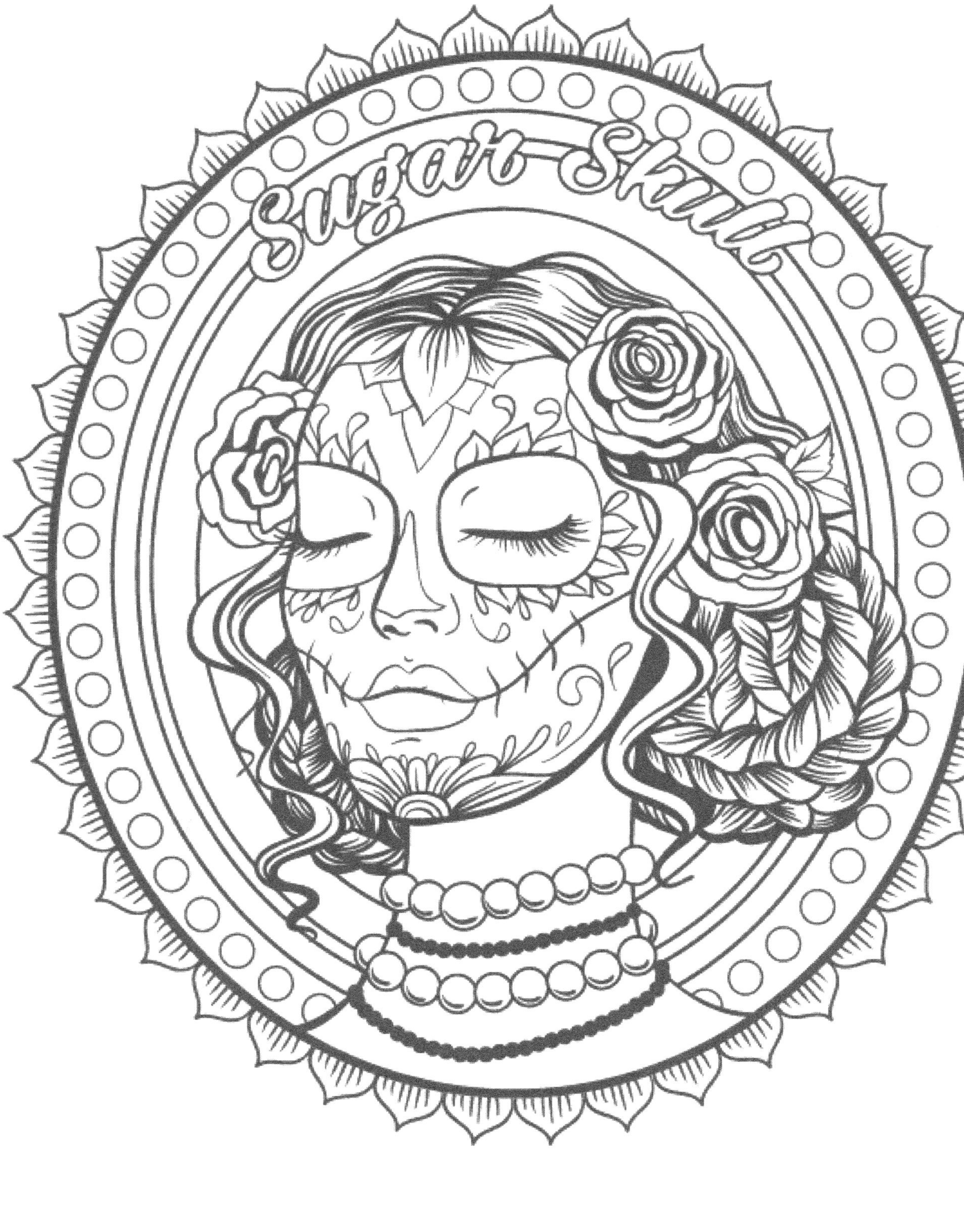
Sugar Skull

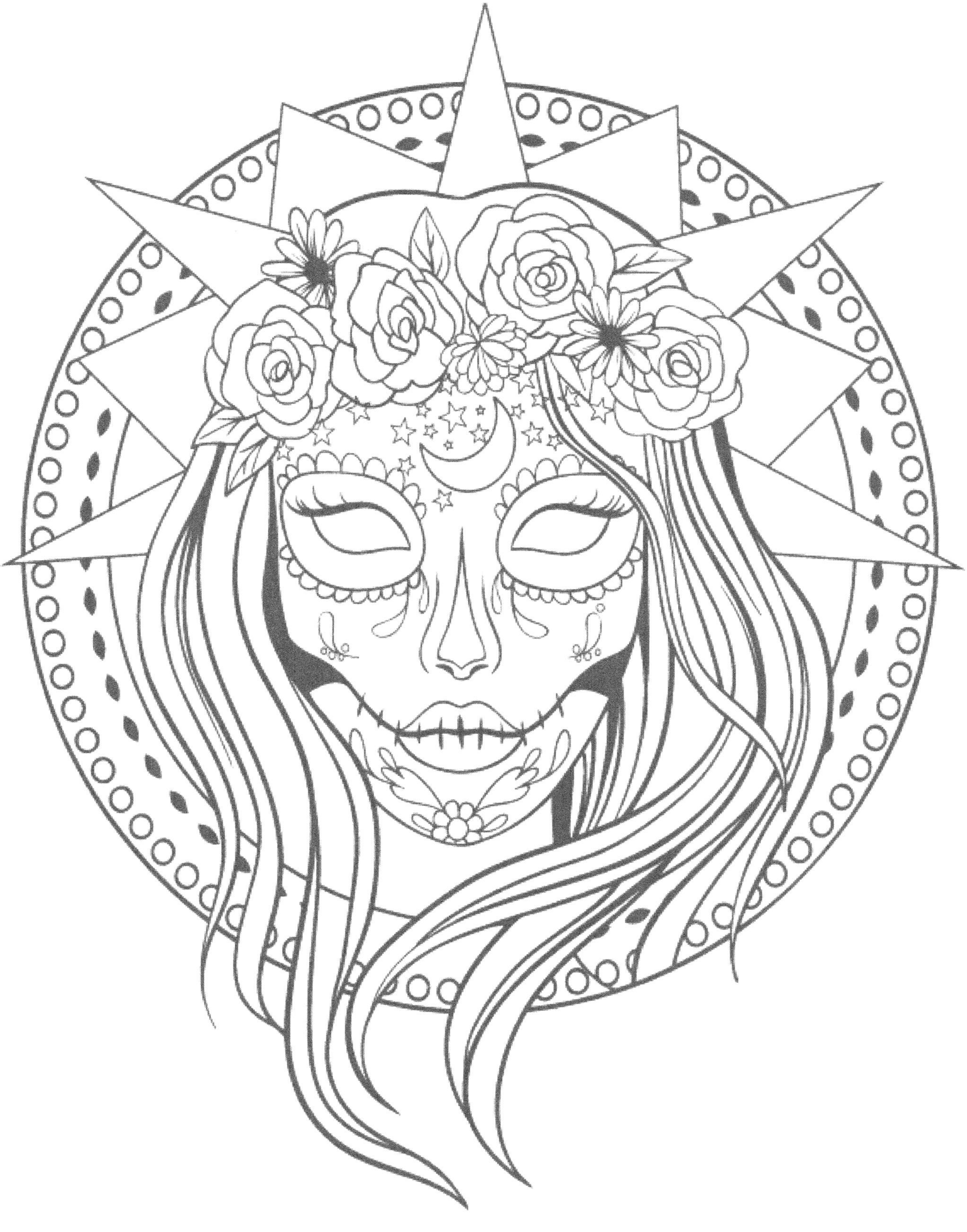

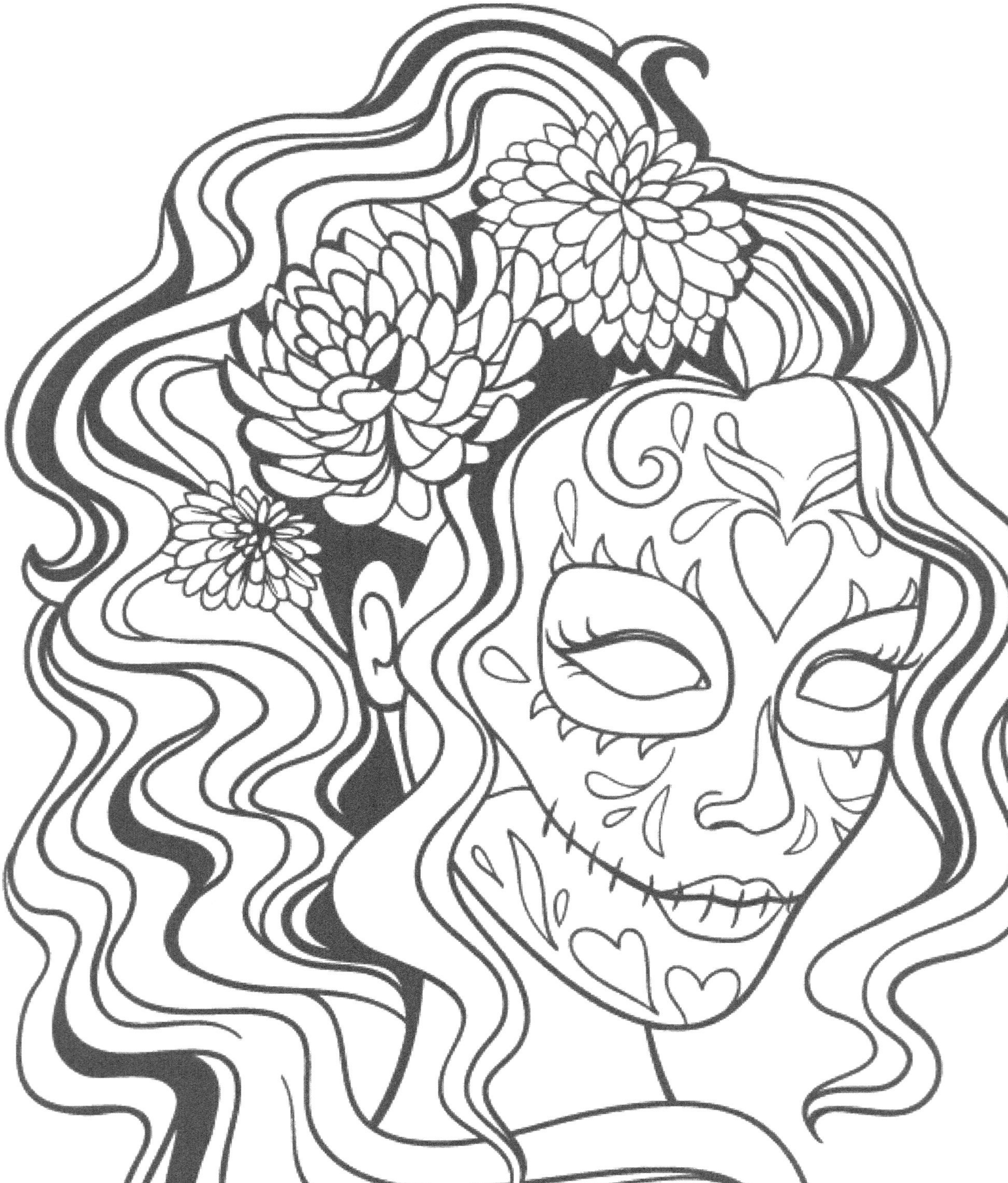

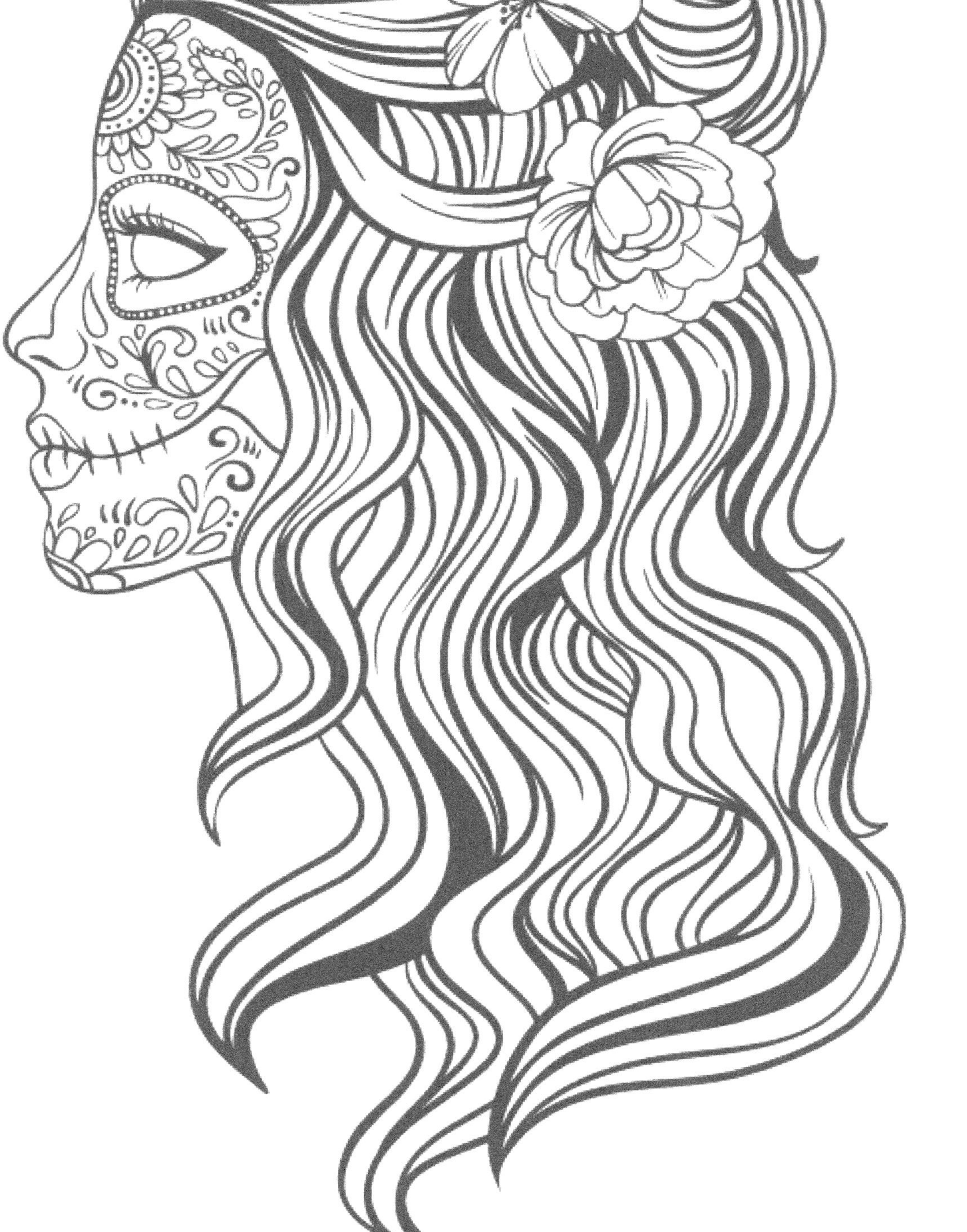

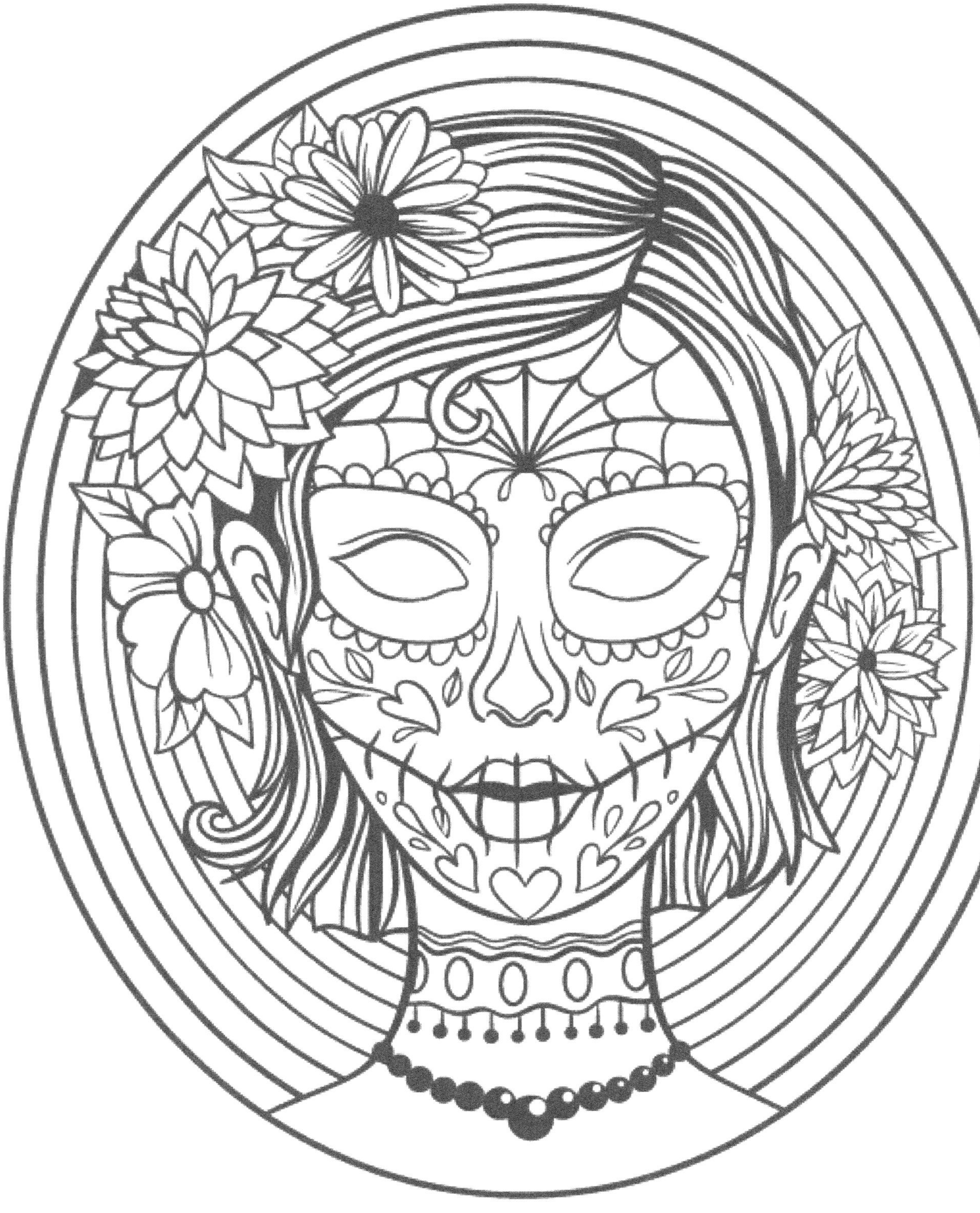

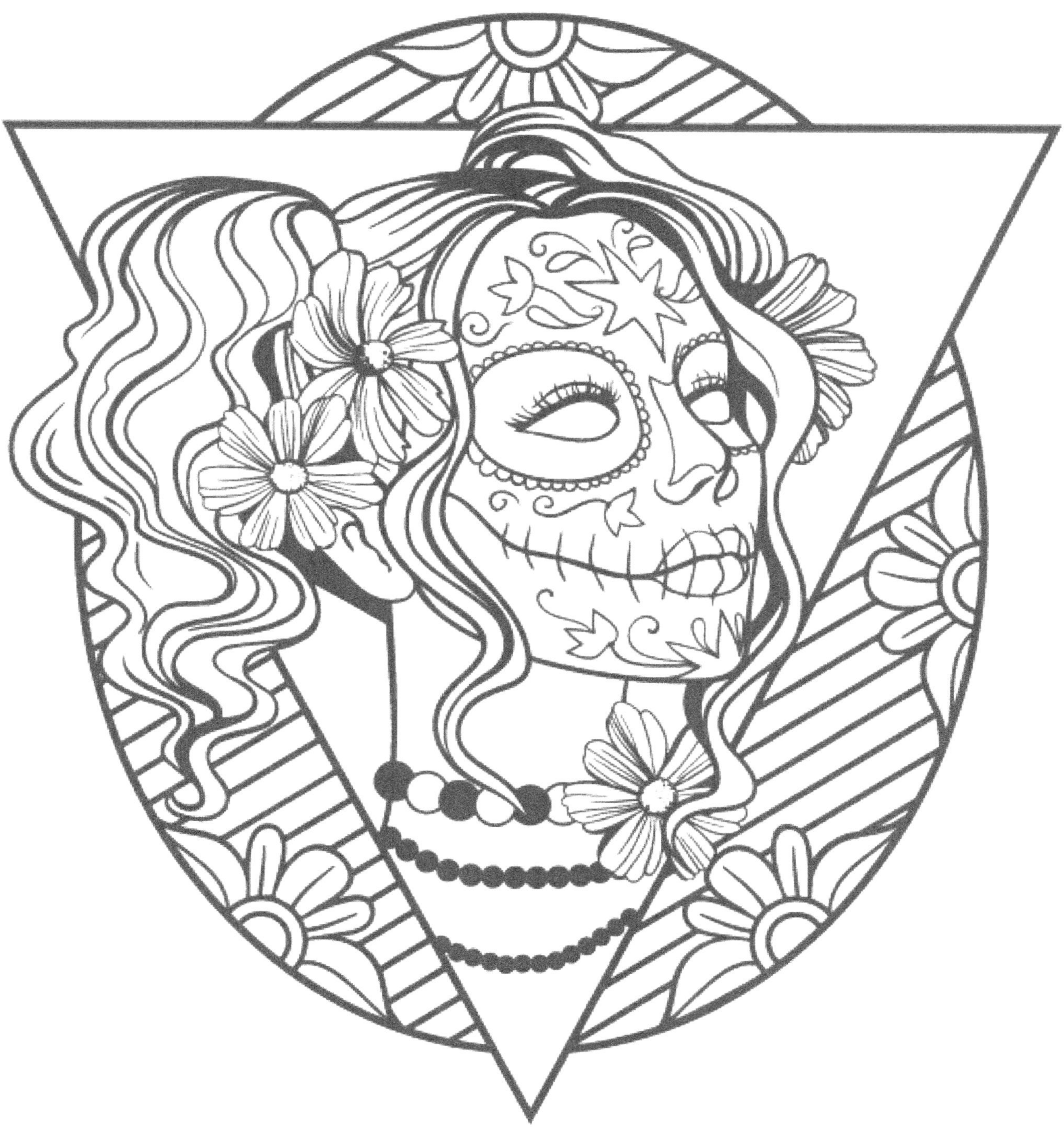

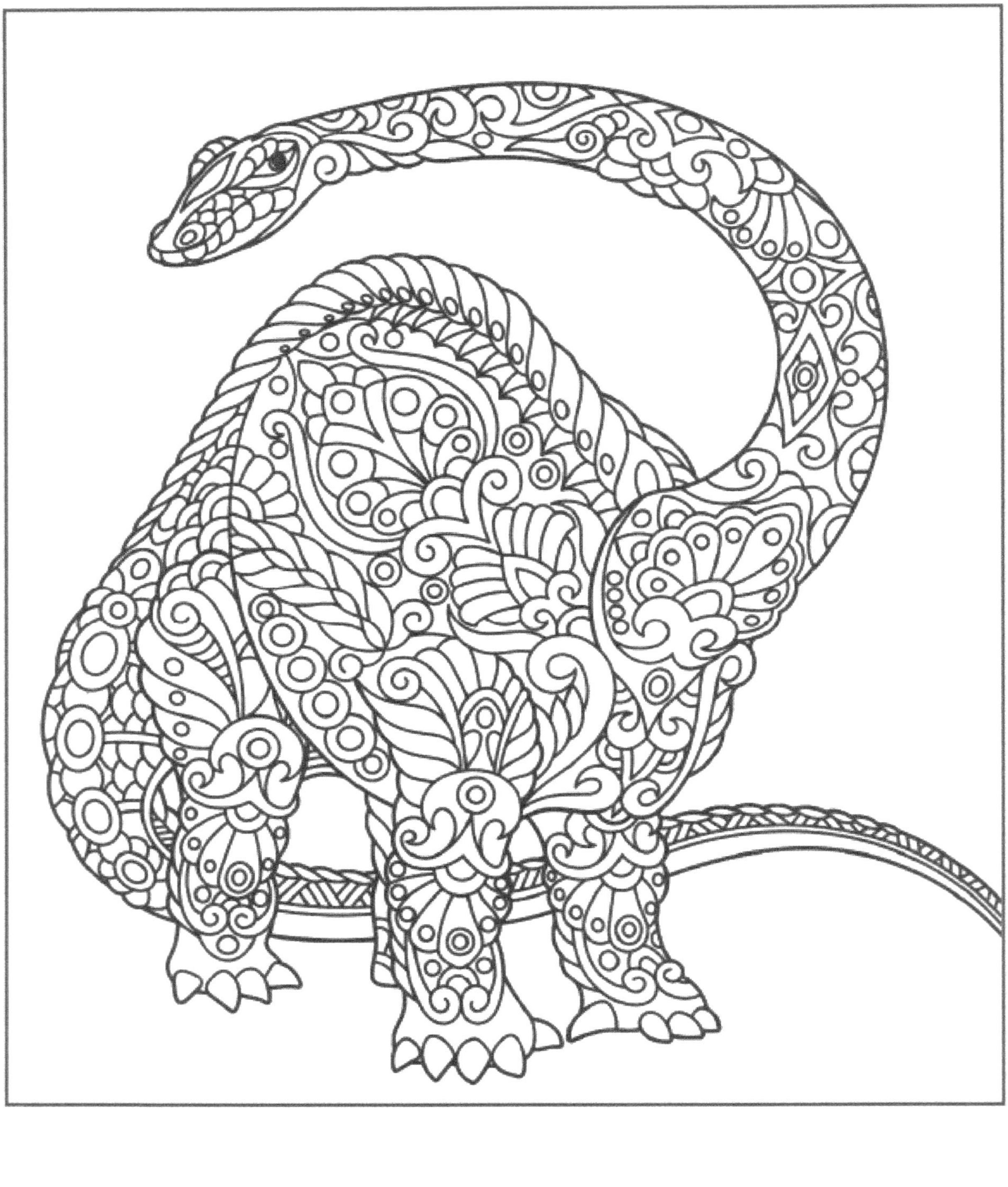

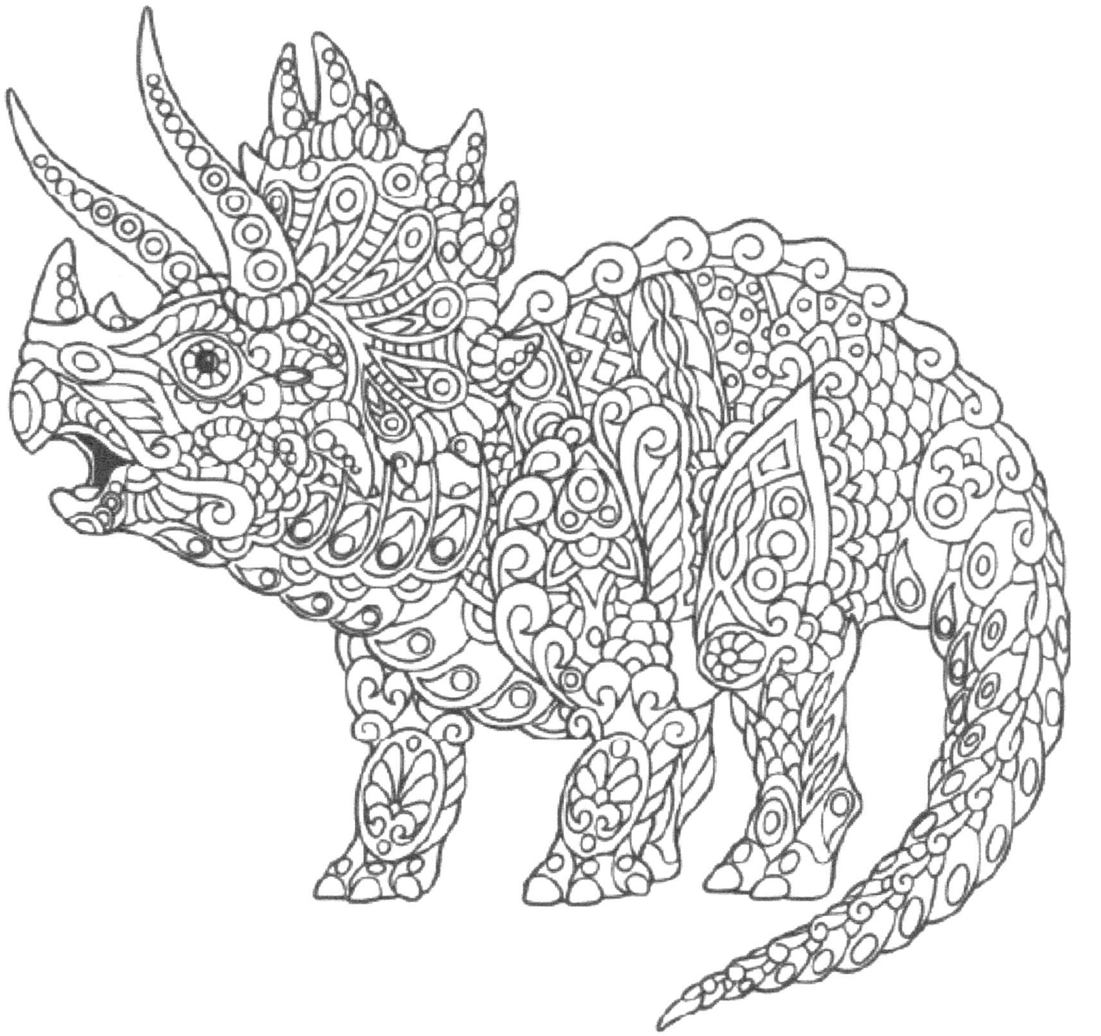

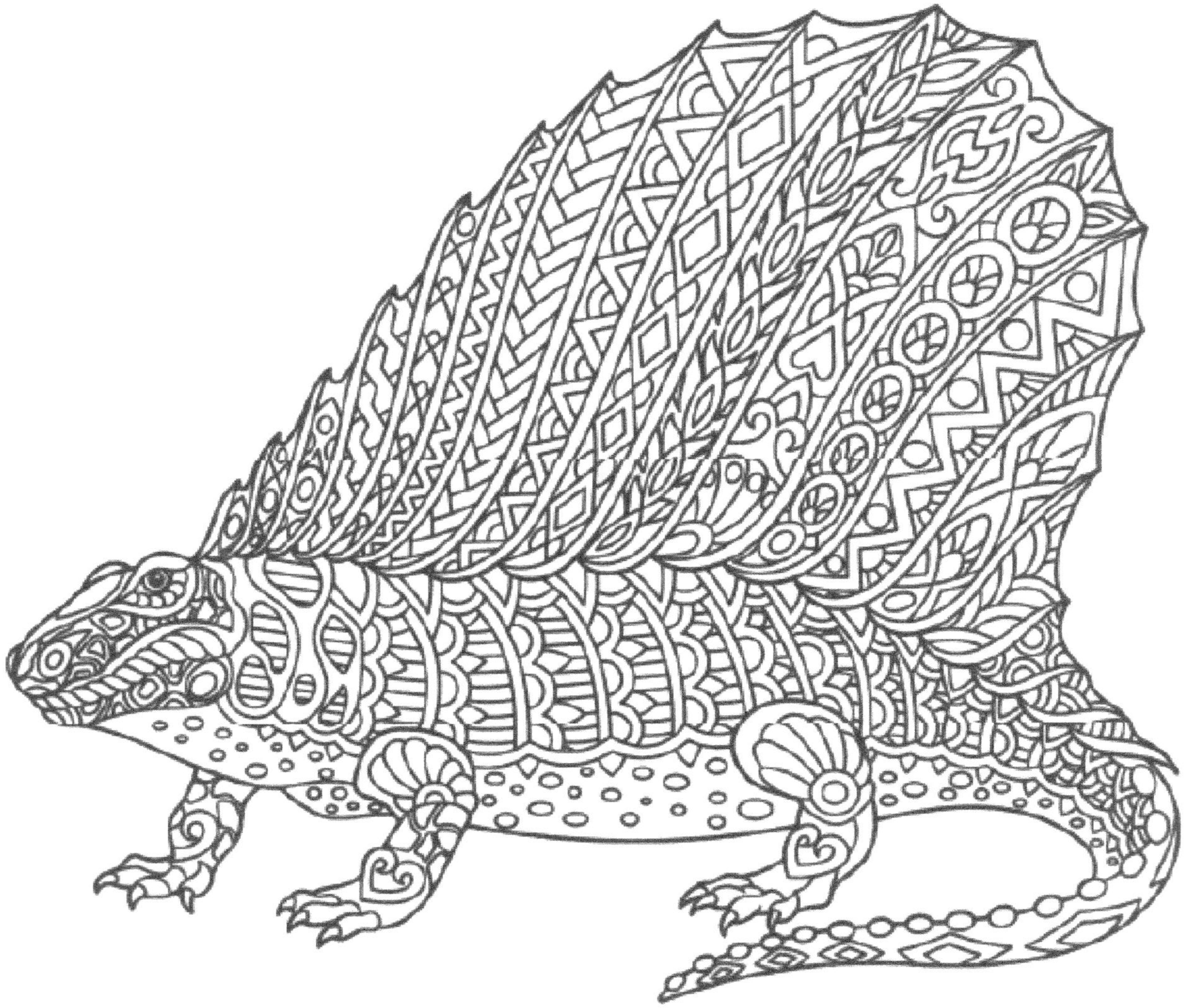

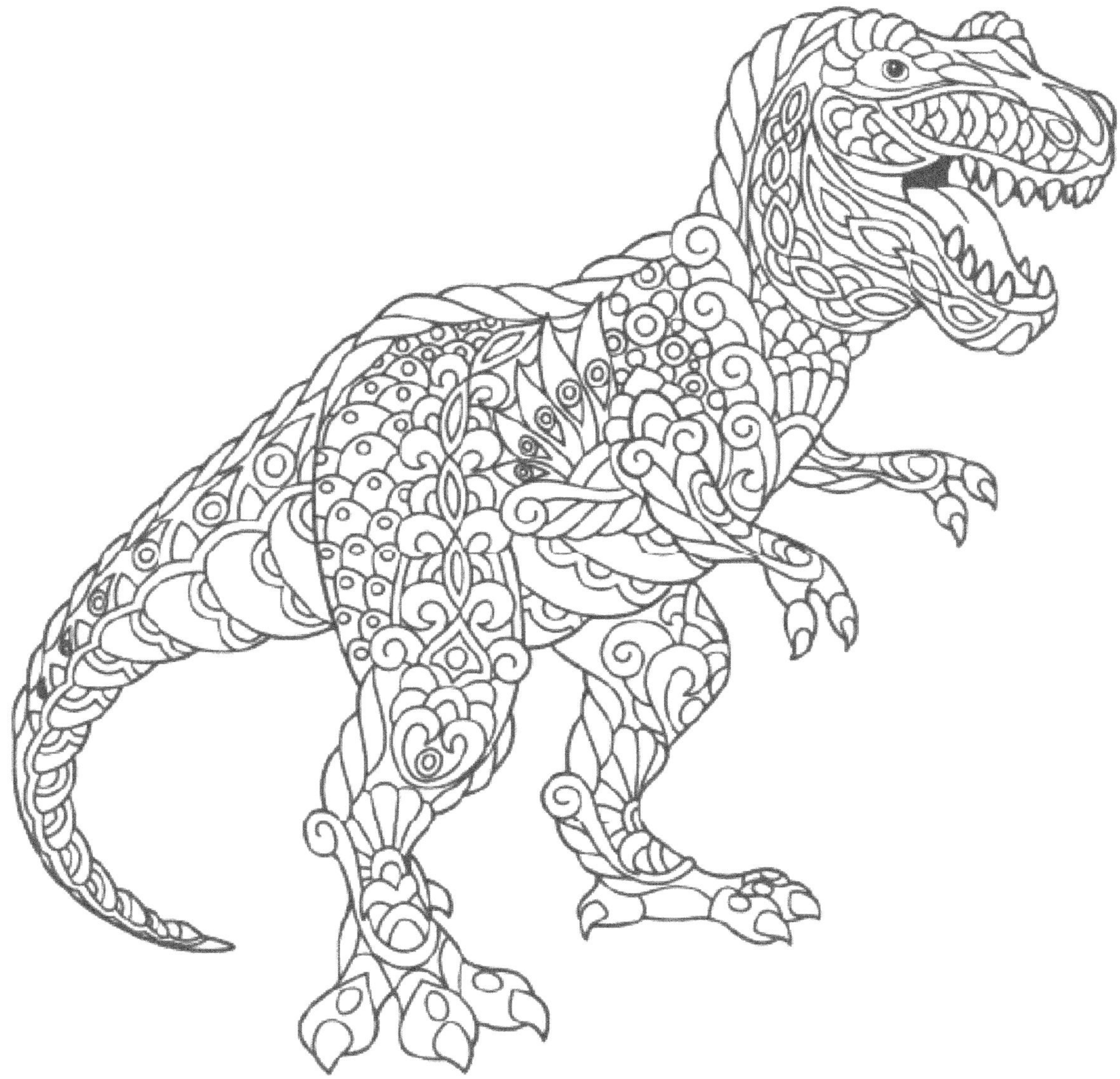

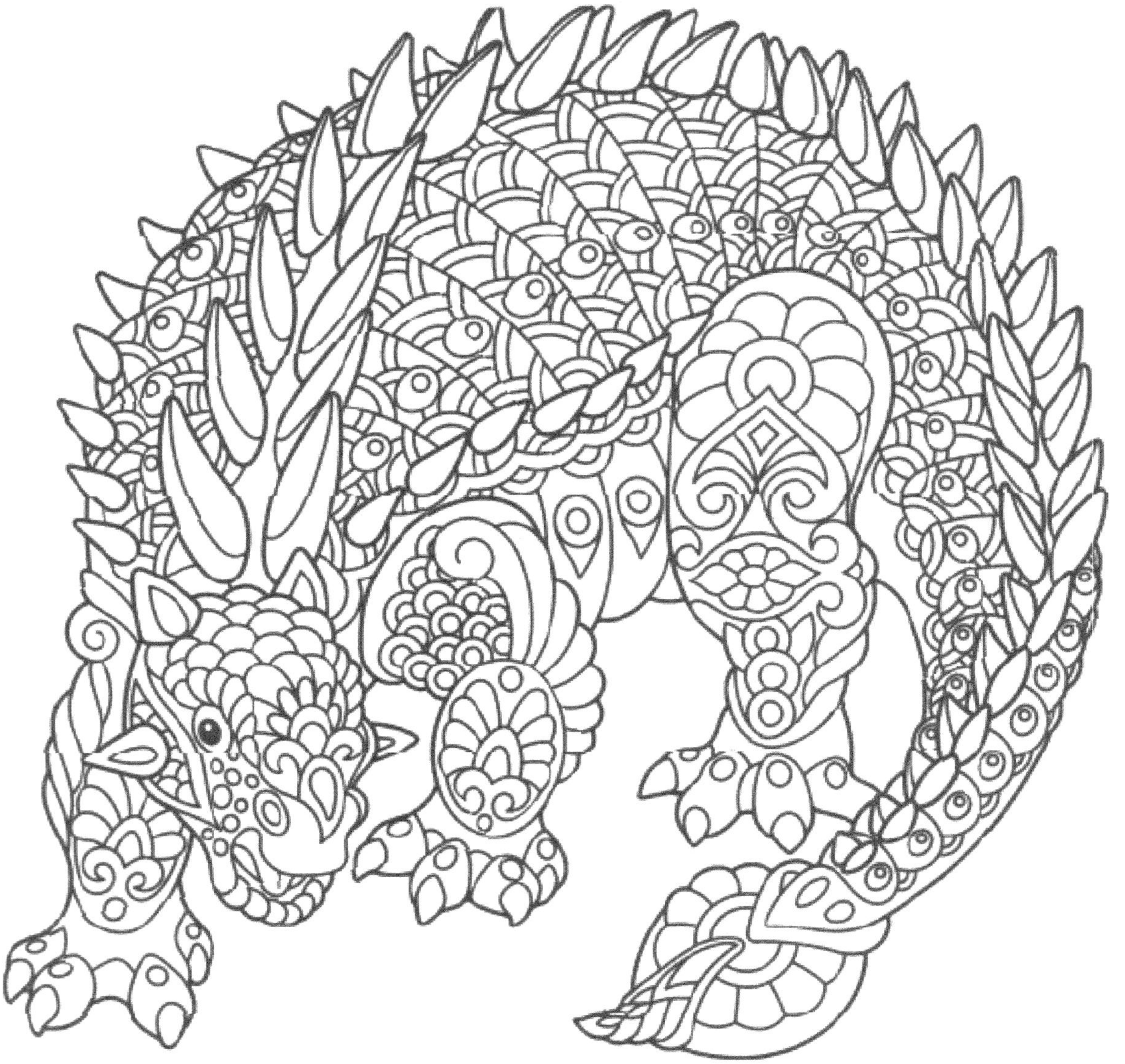

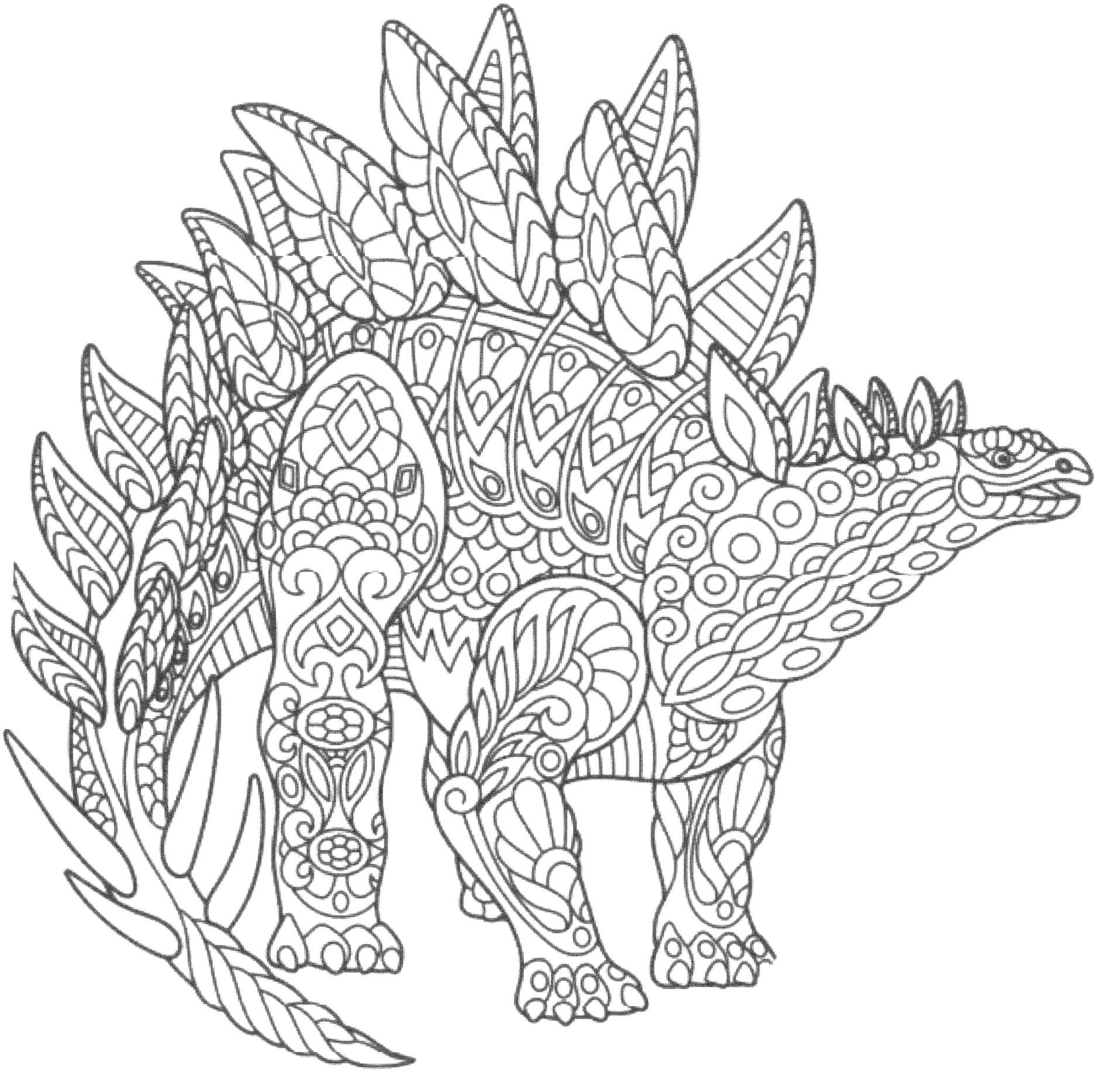

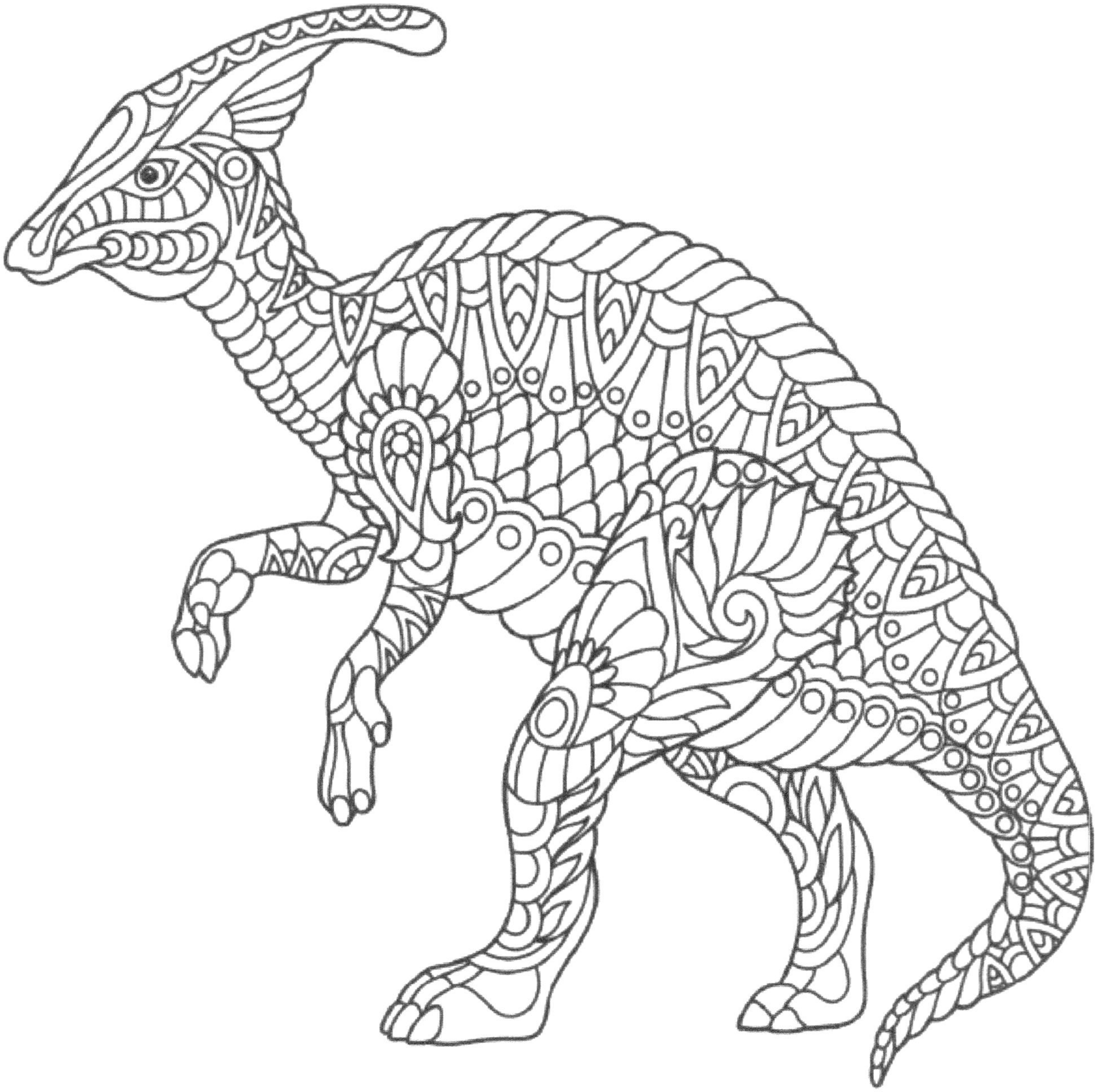

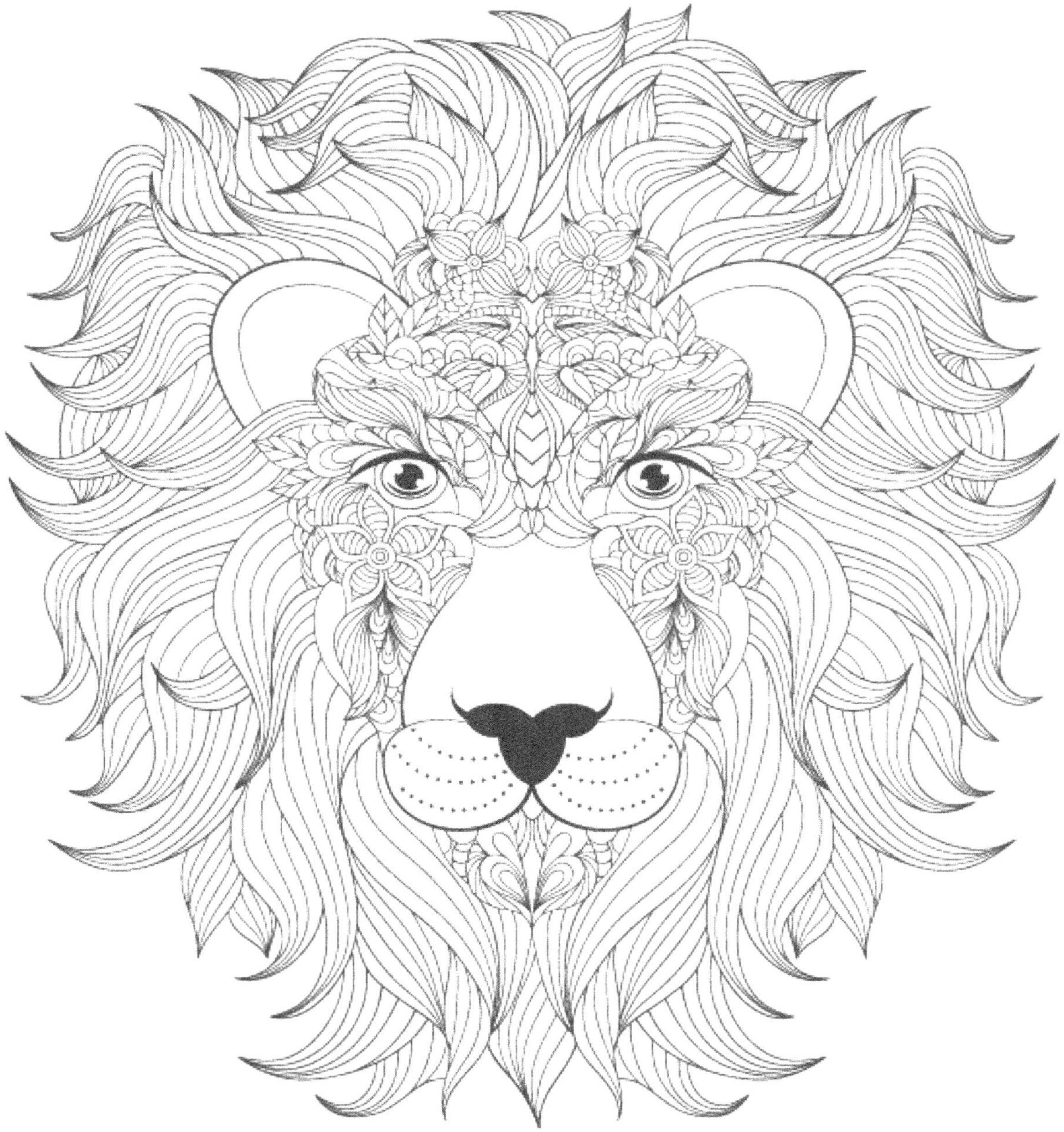

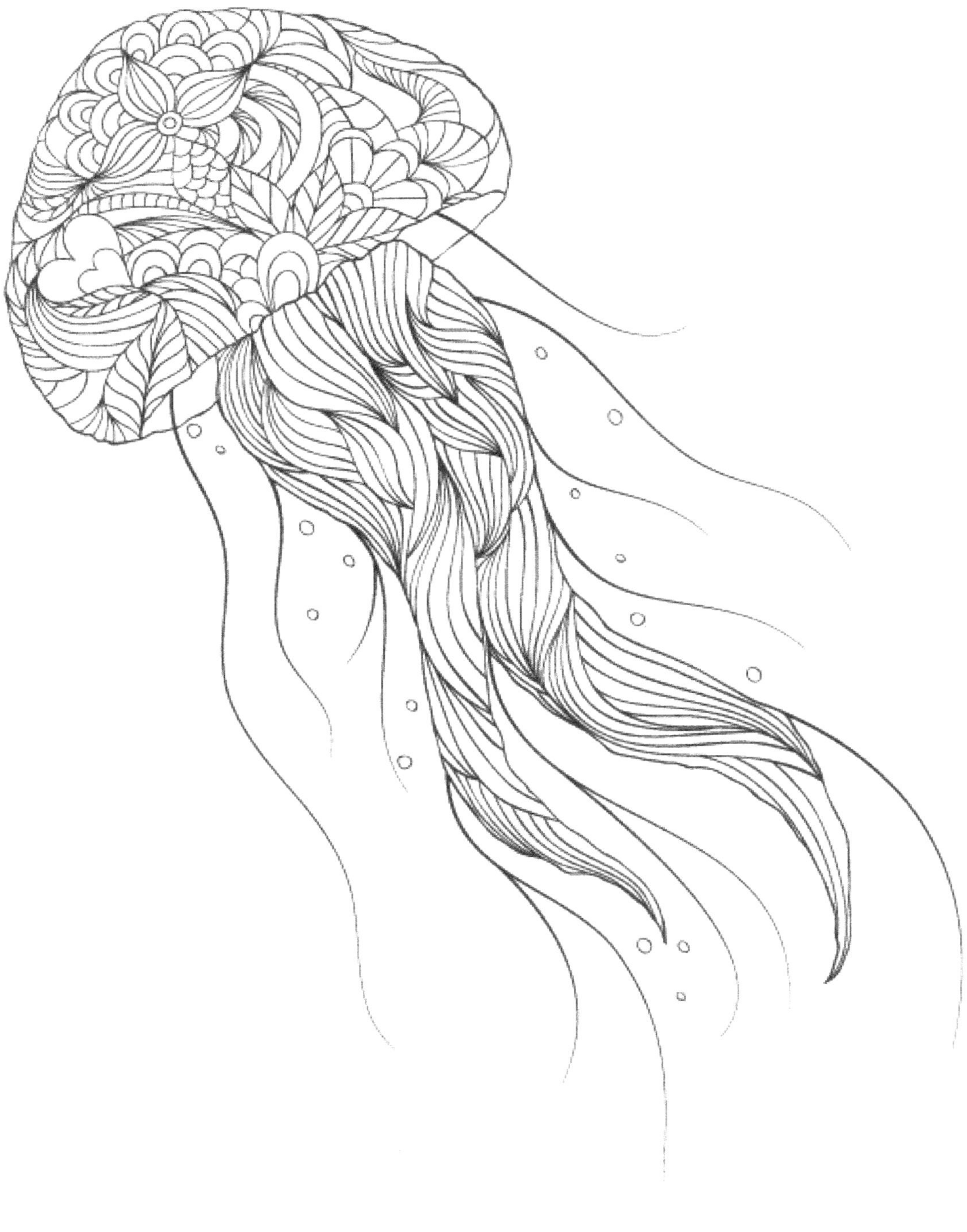

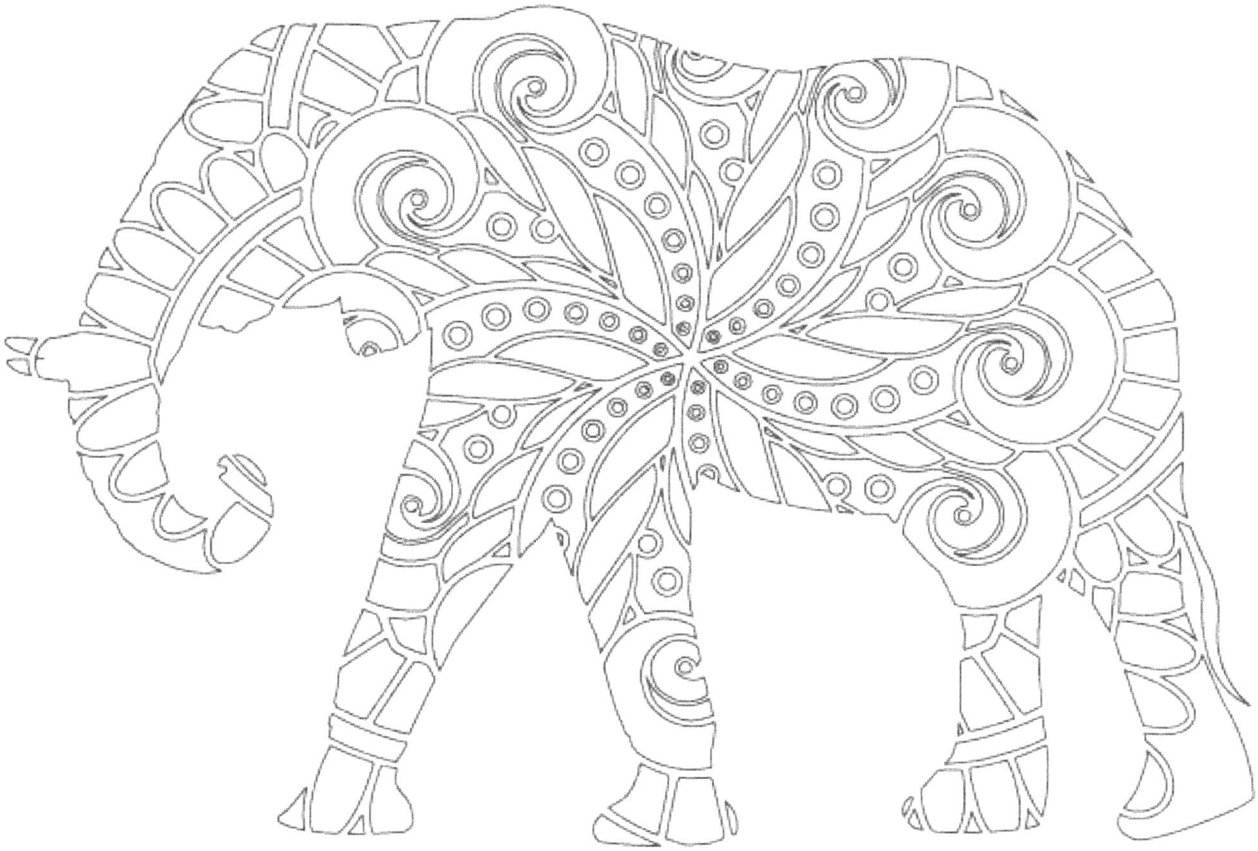

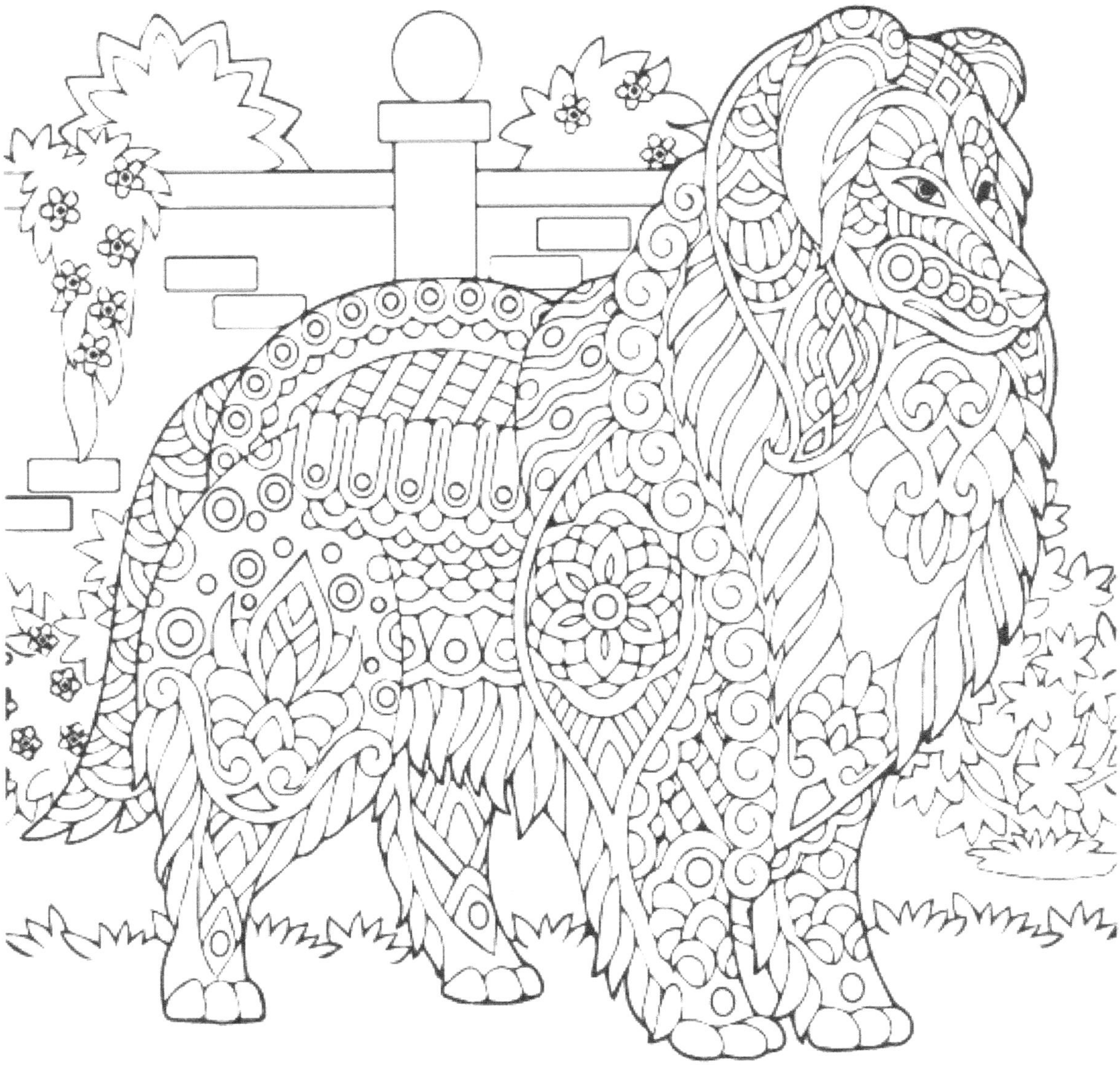

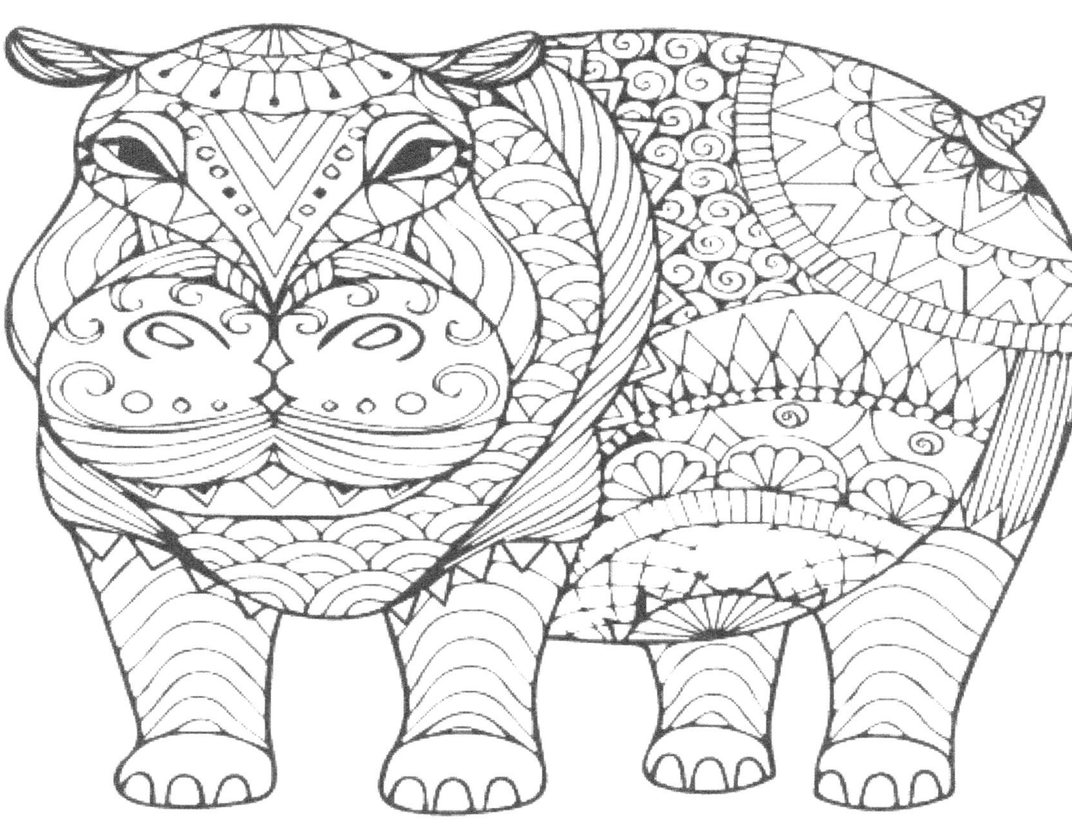

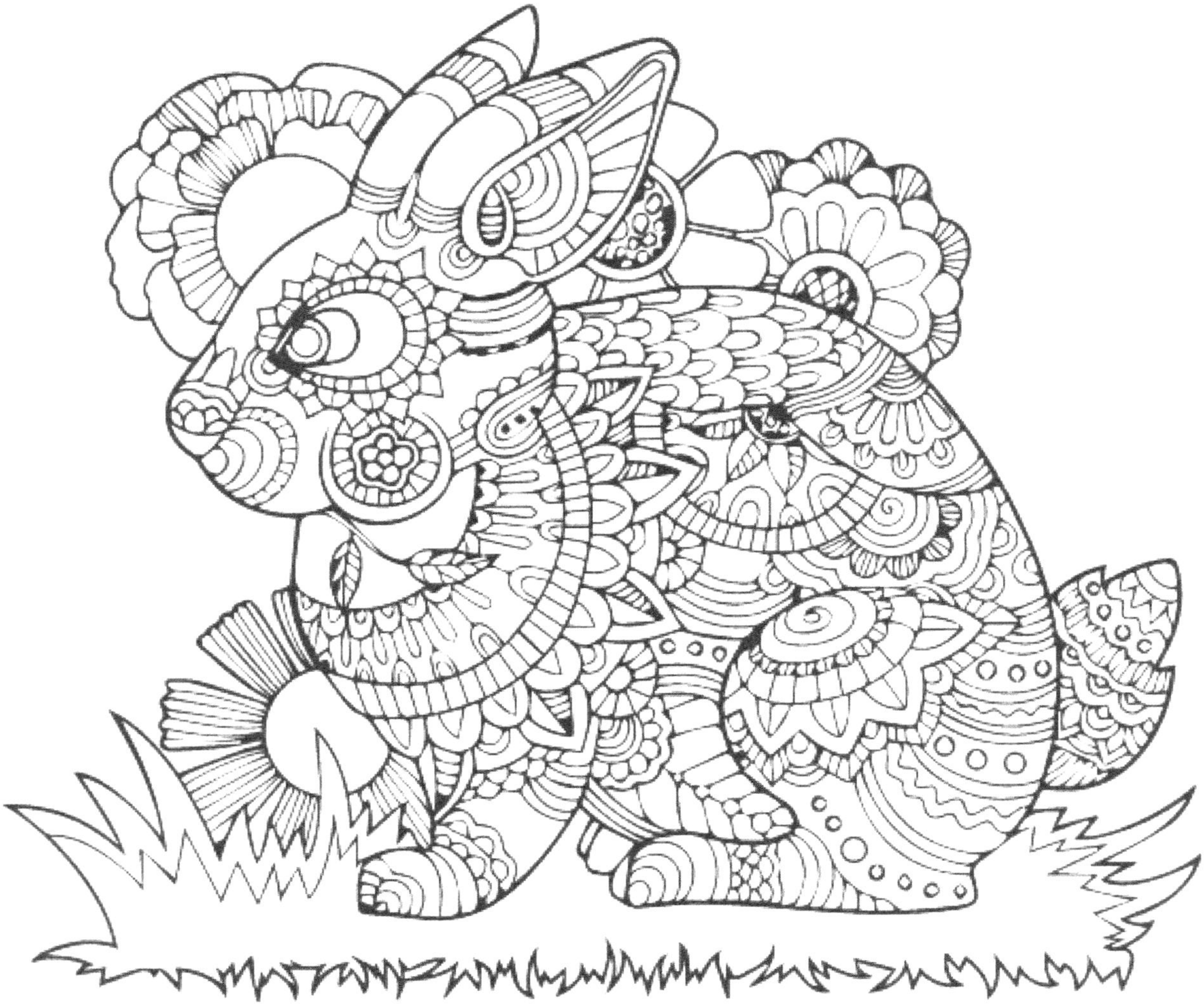

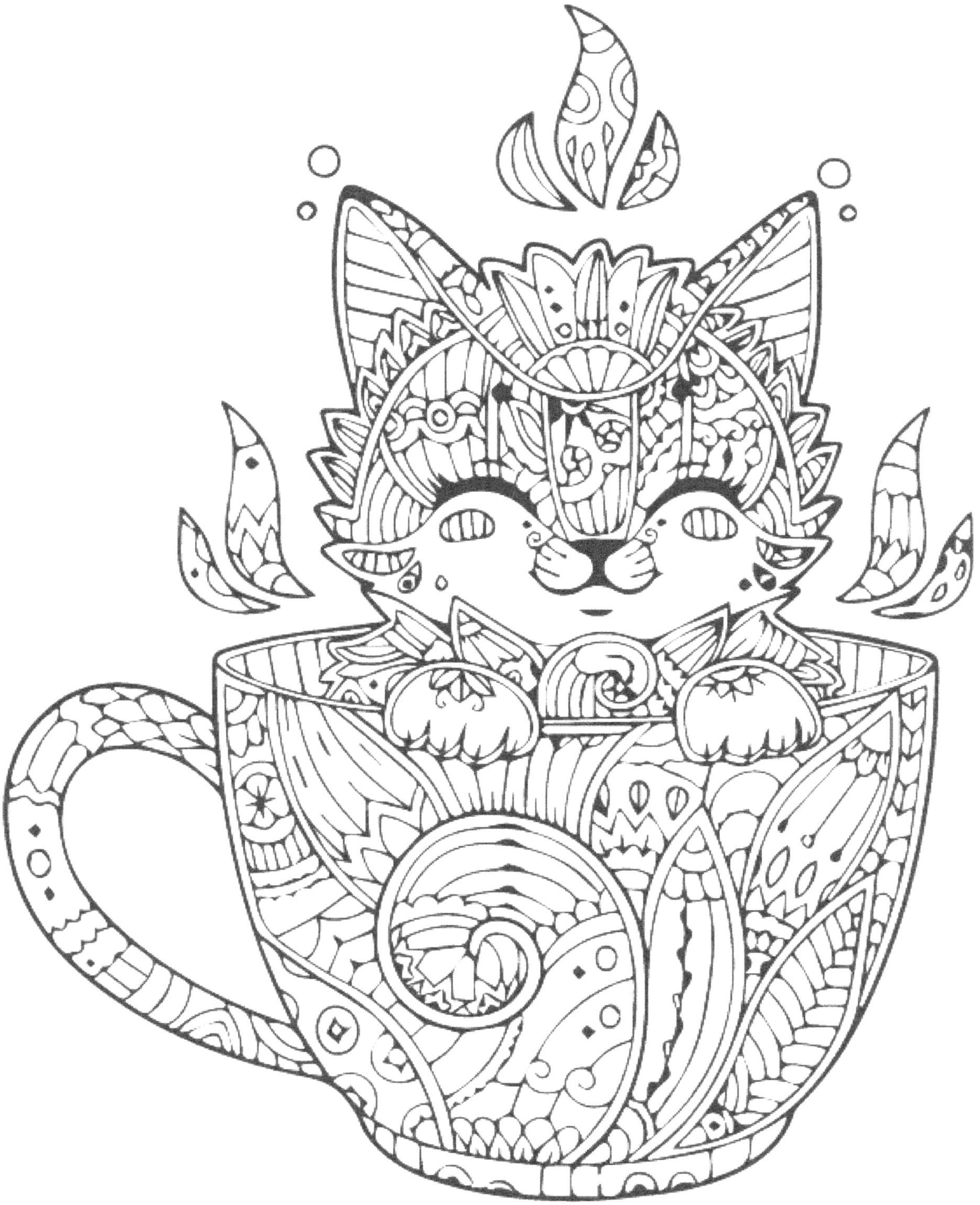

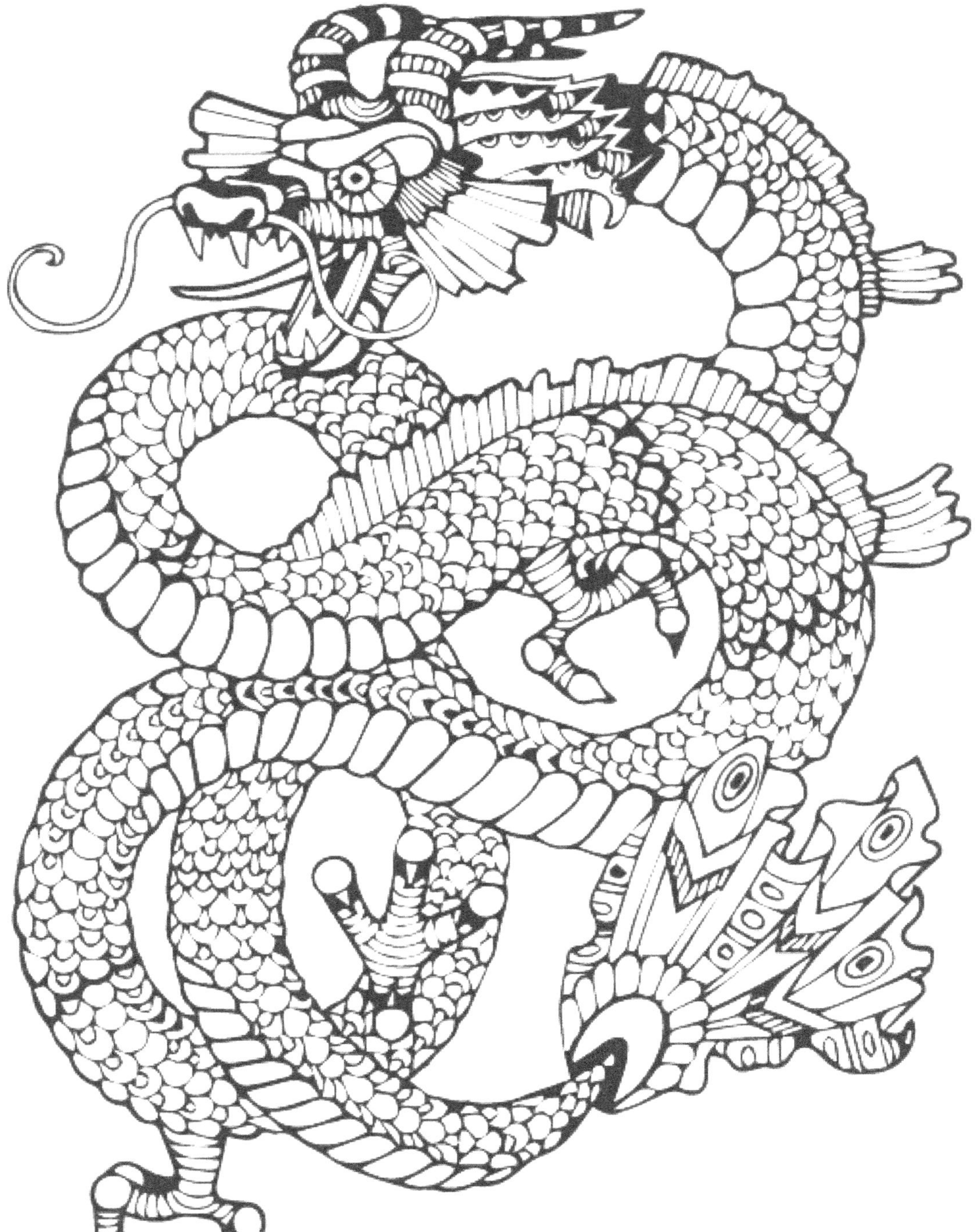

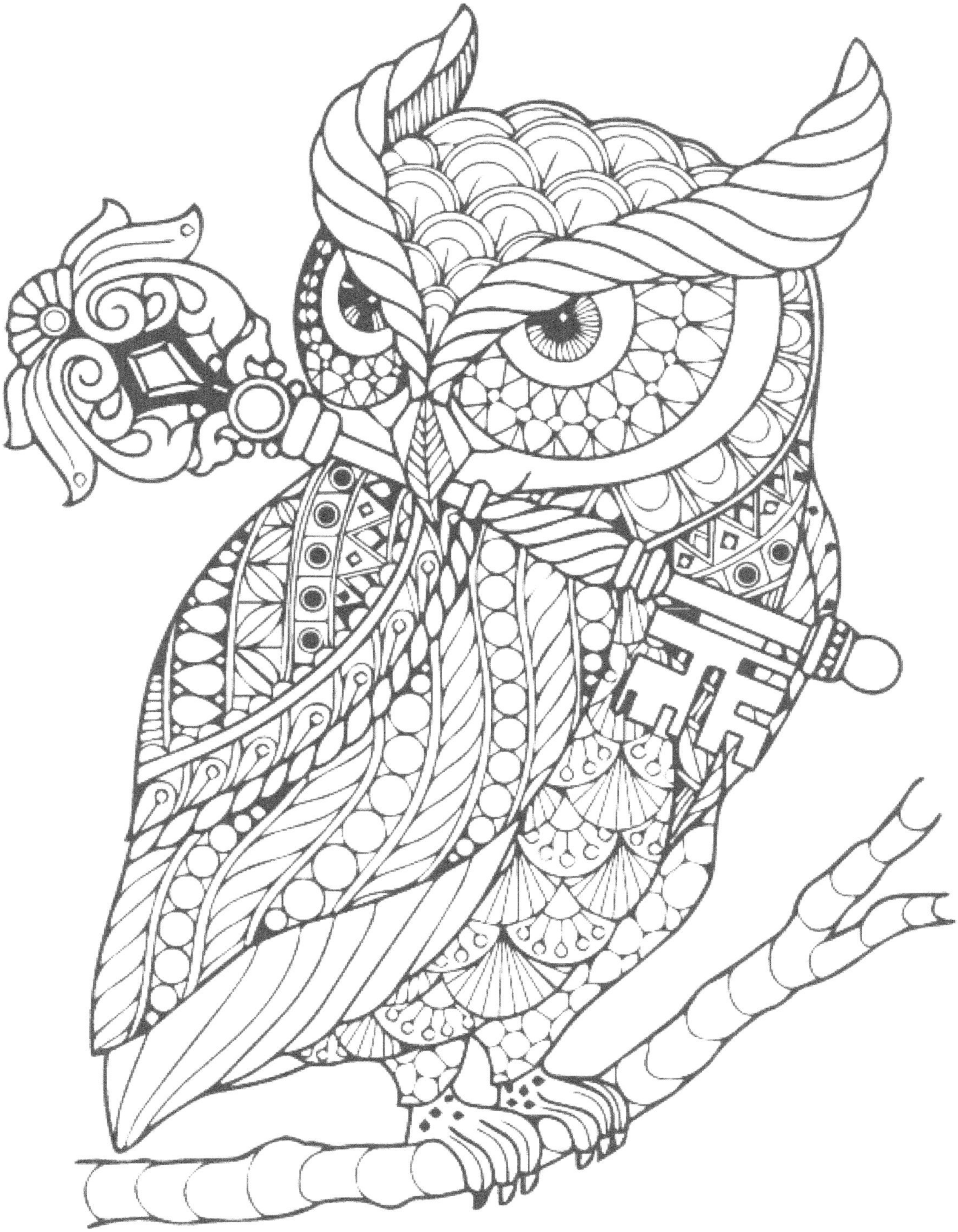

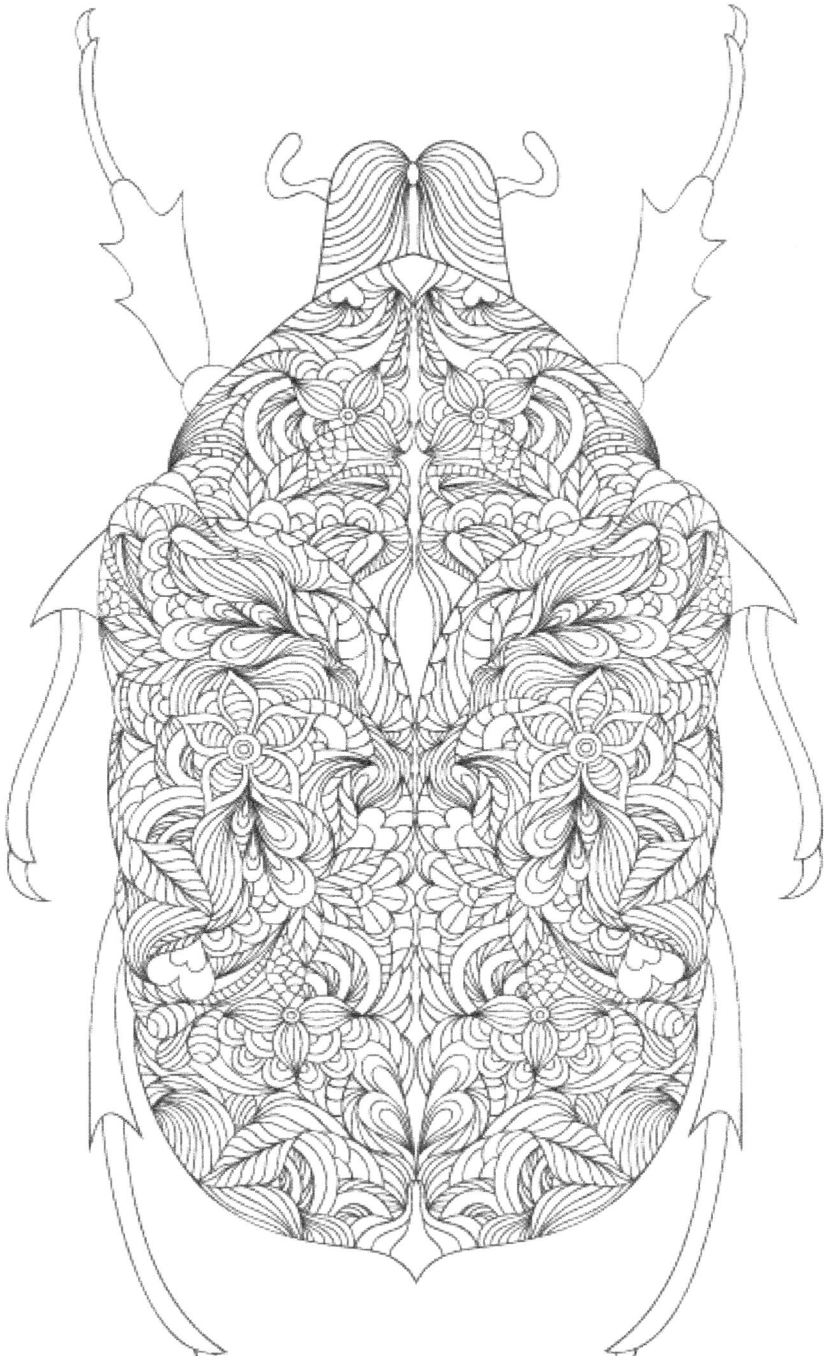

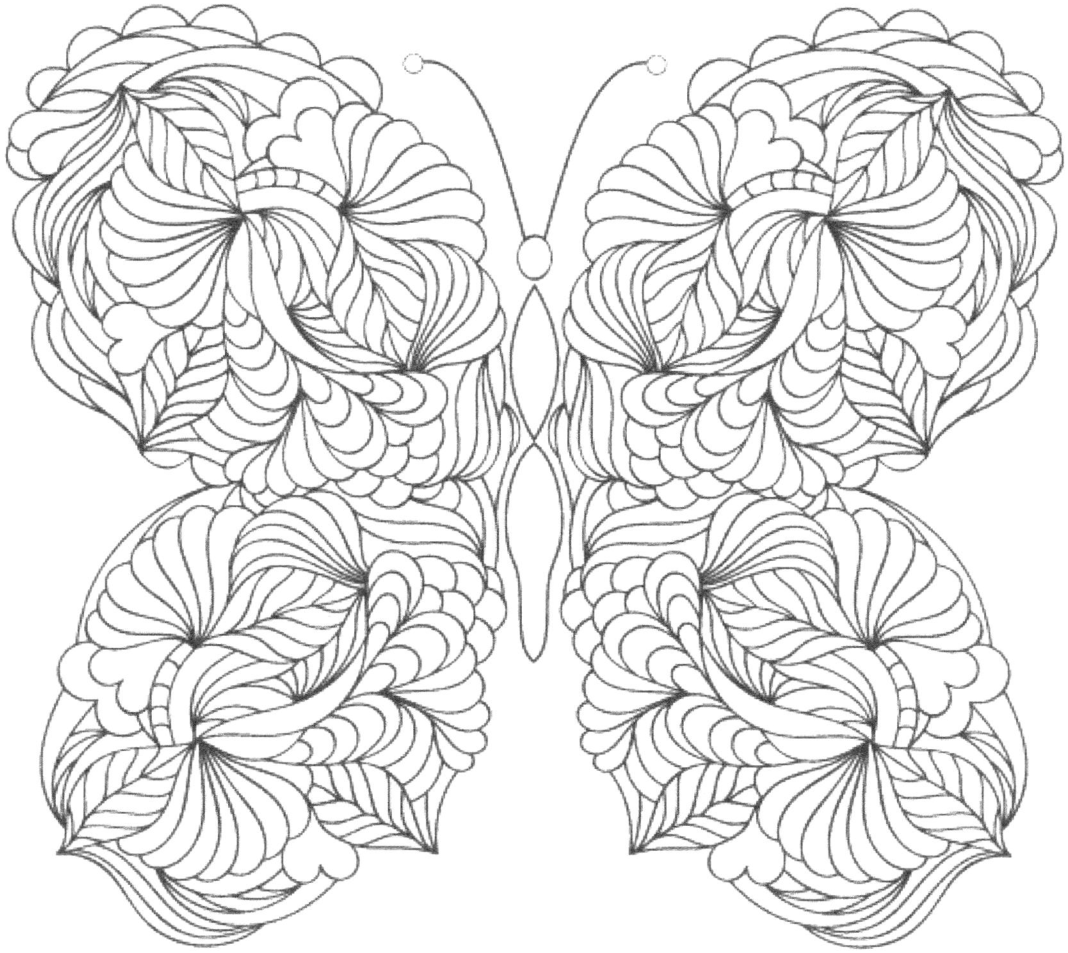

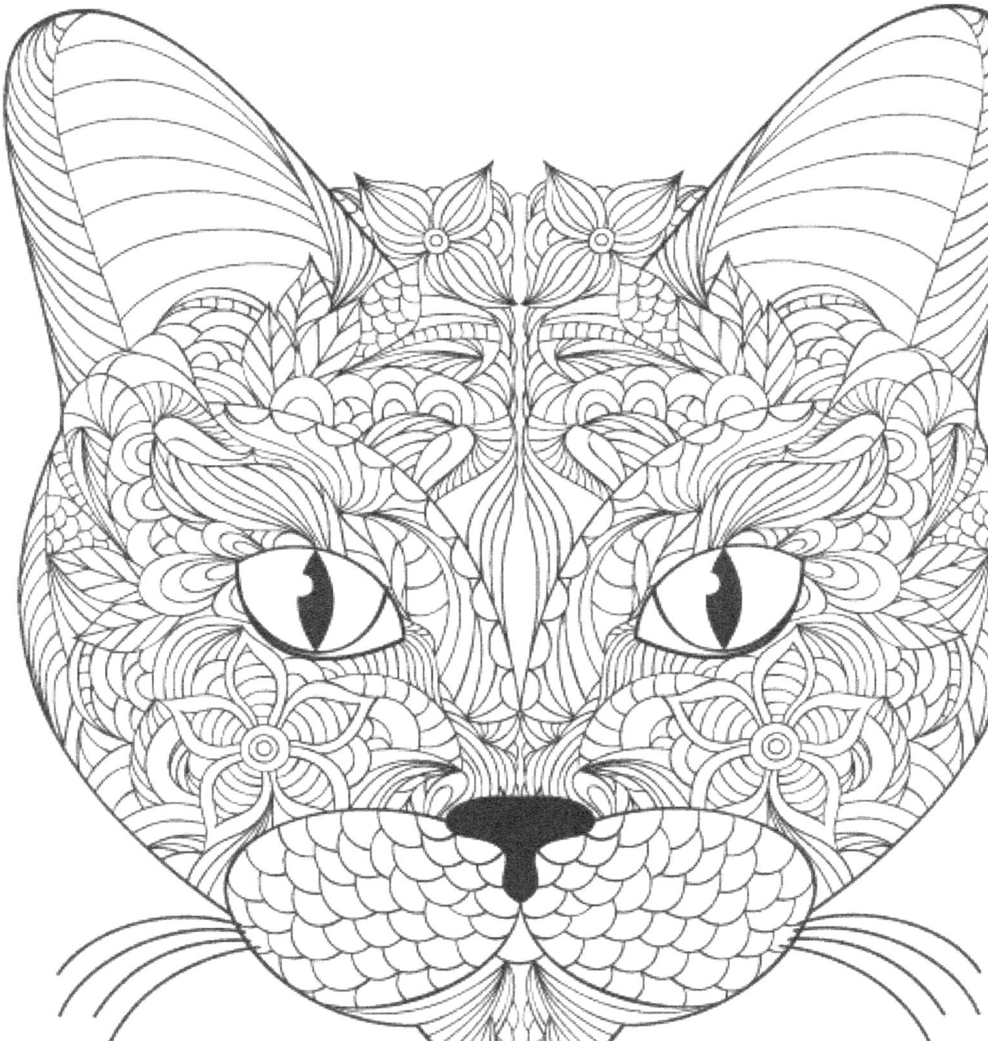

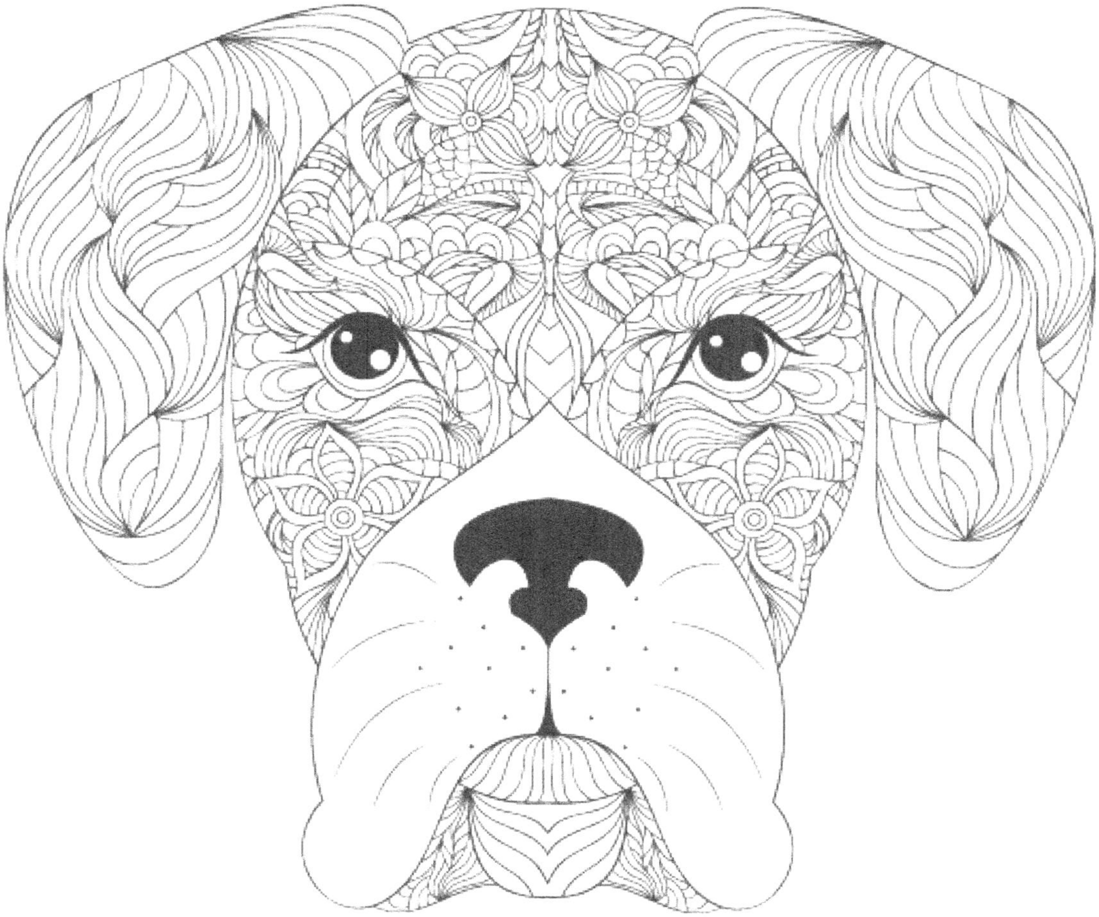

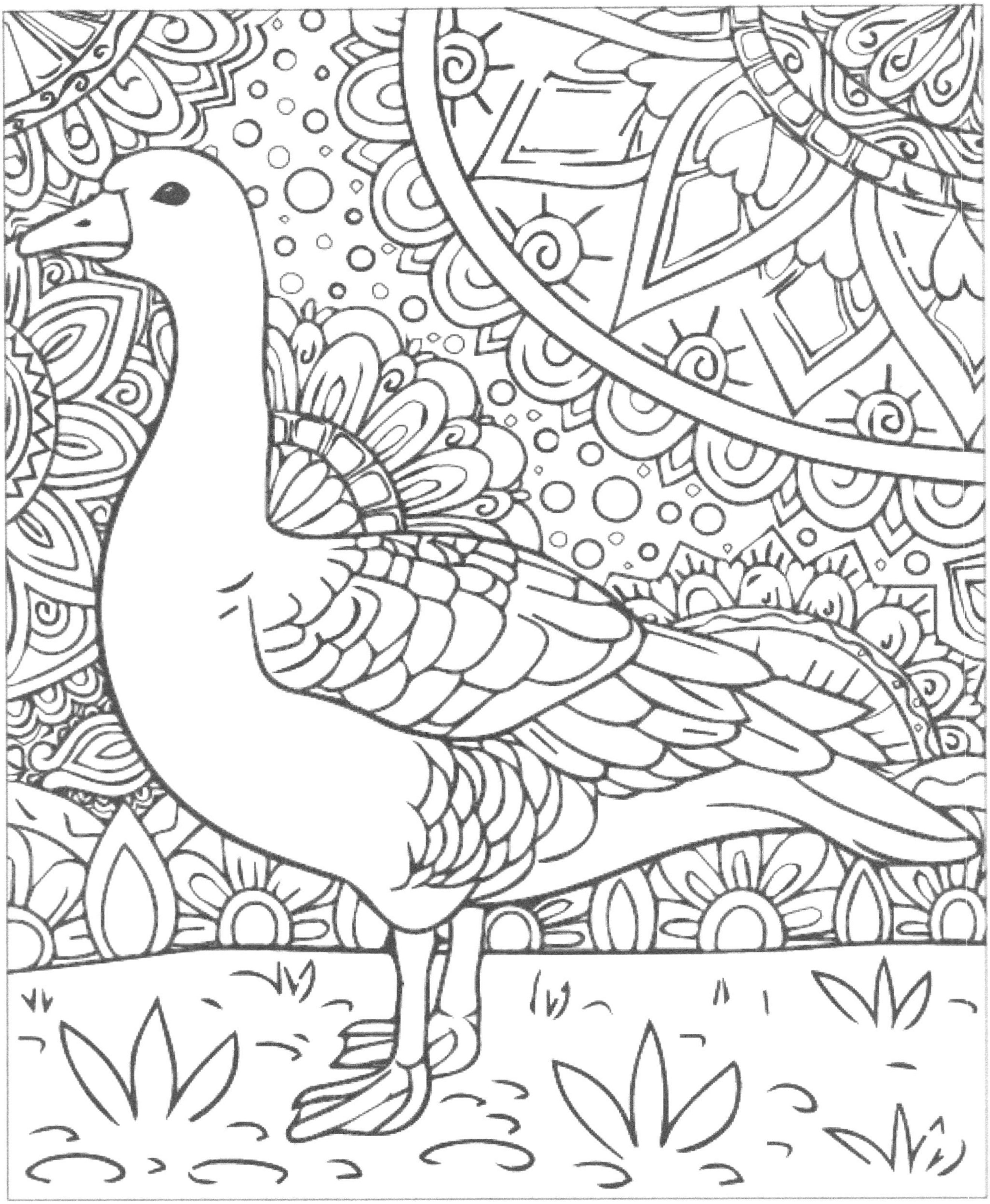

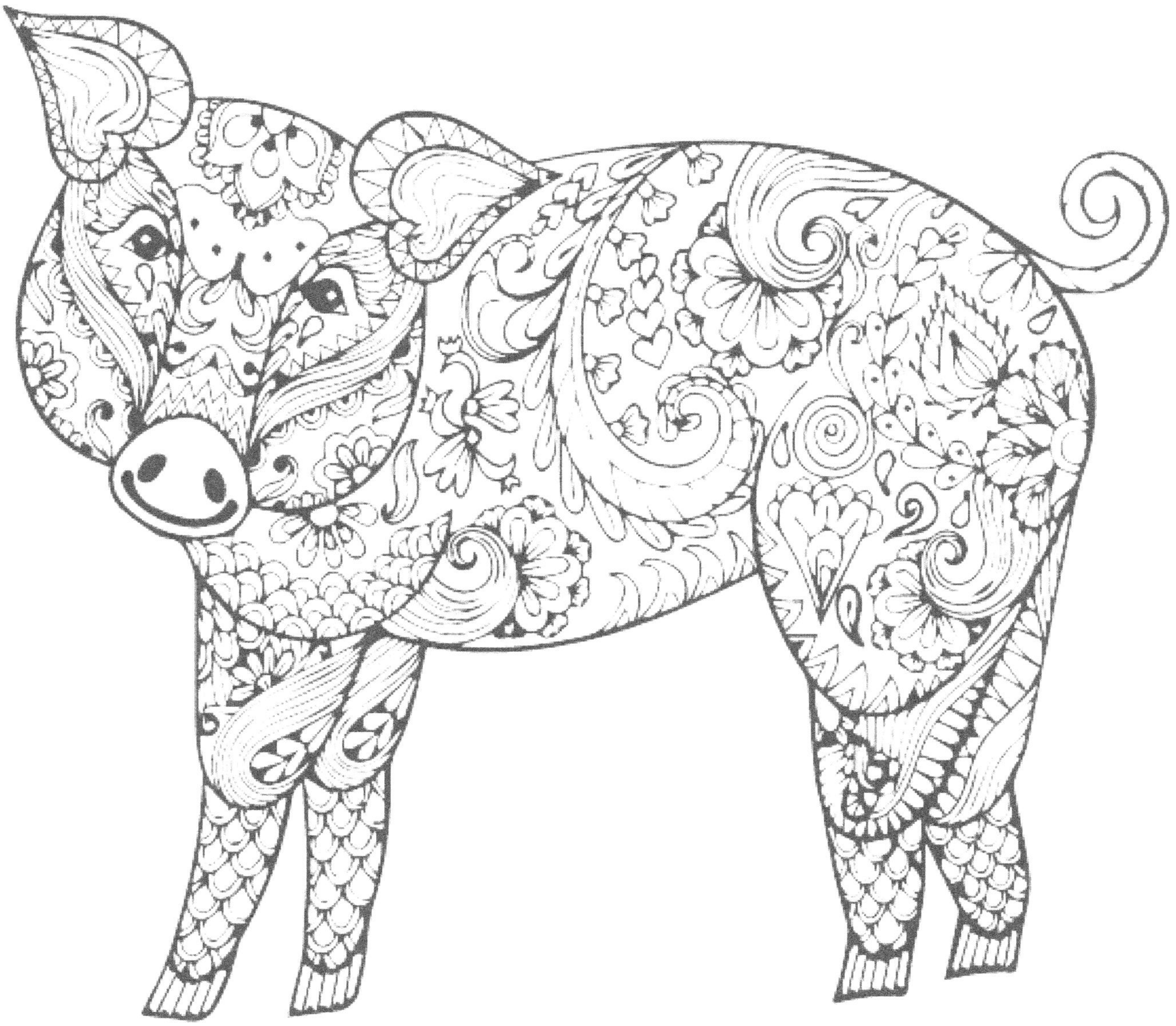

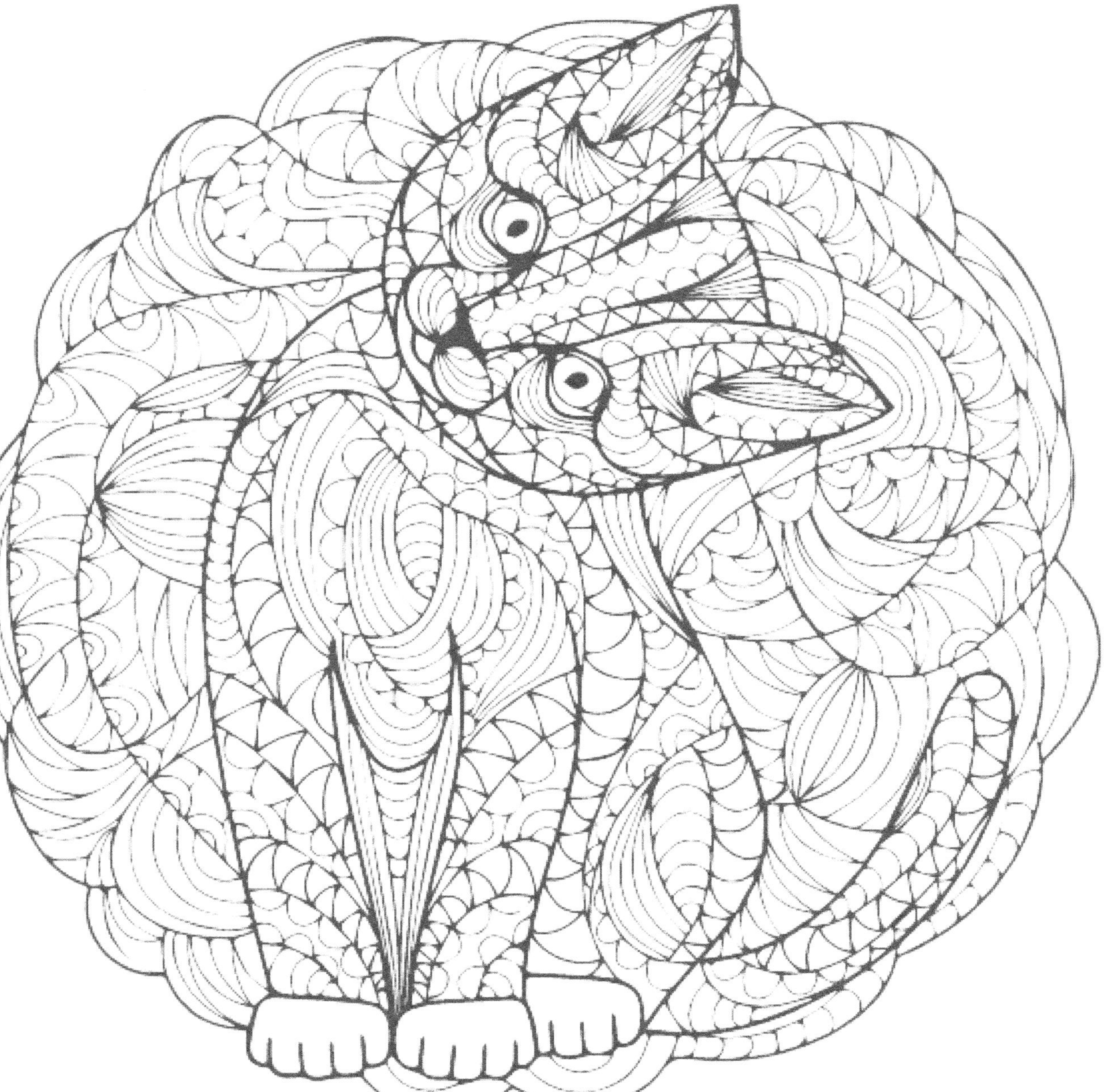

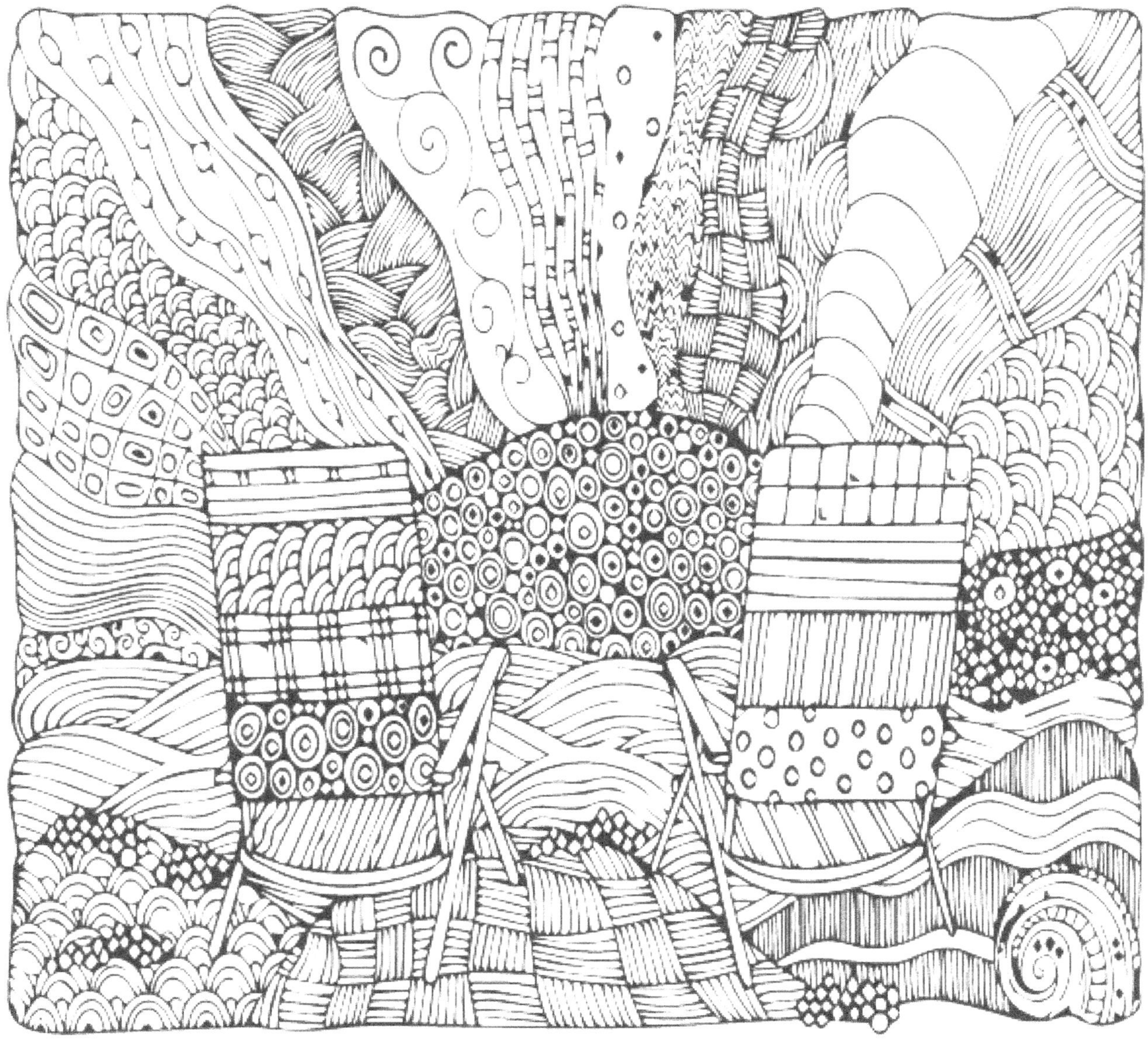

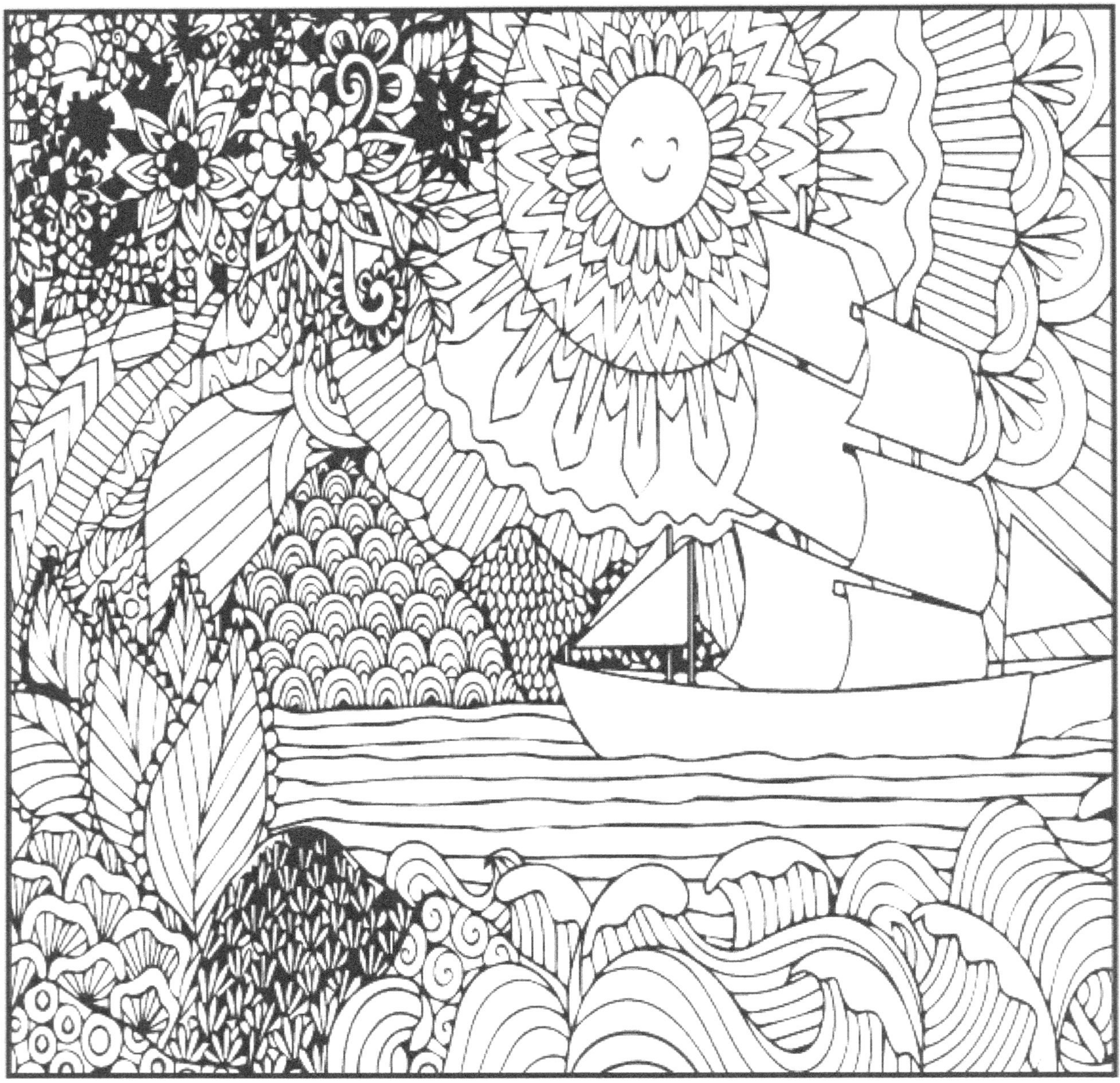

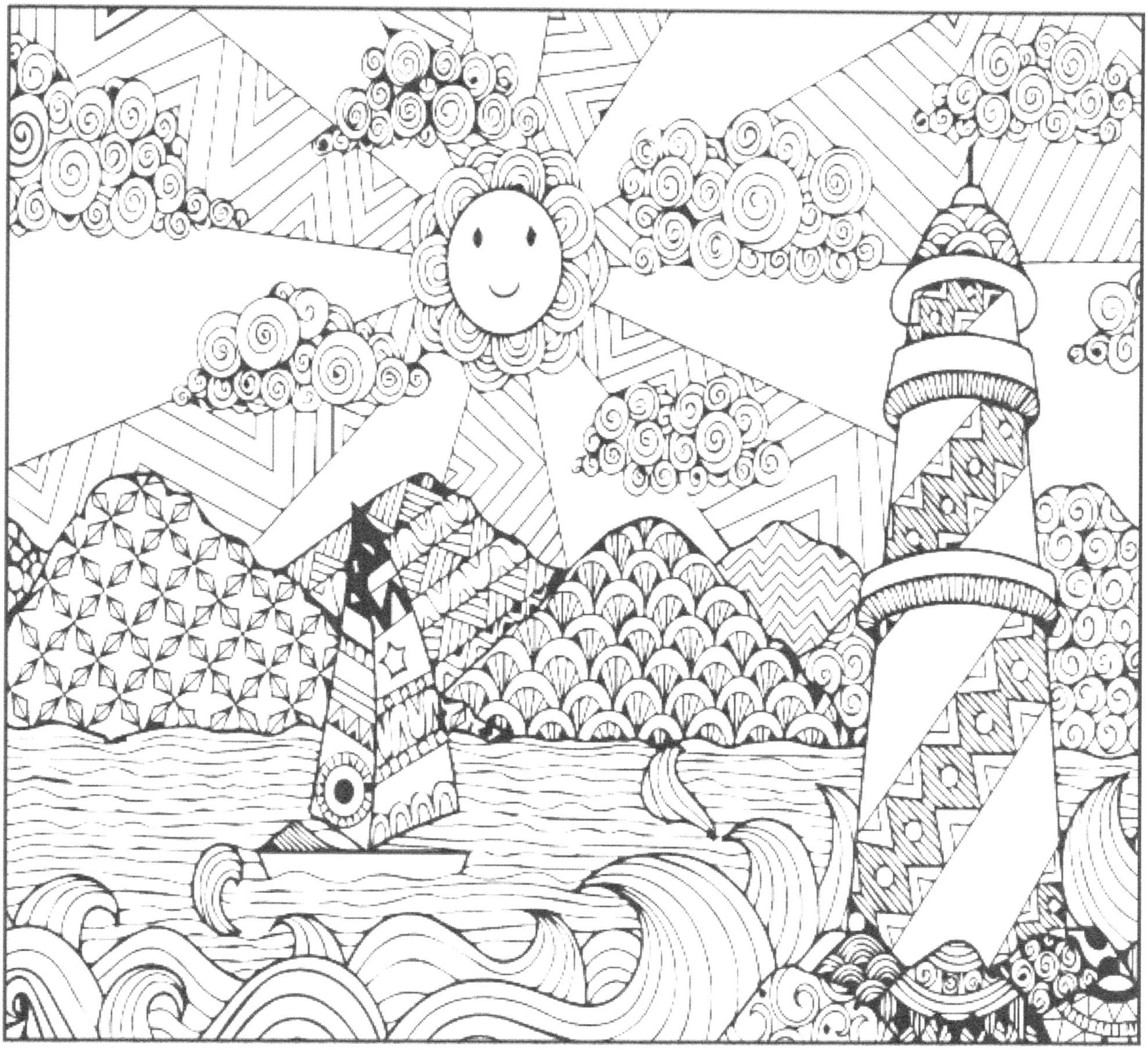

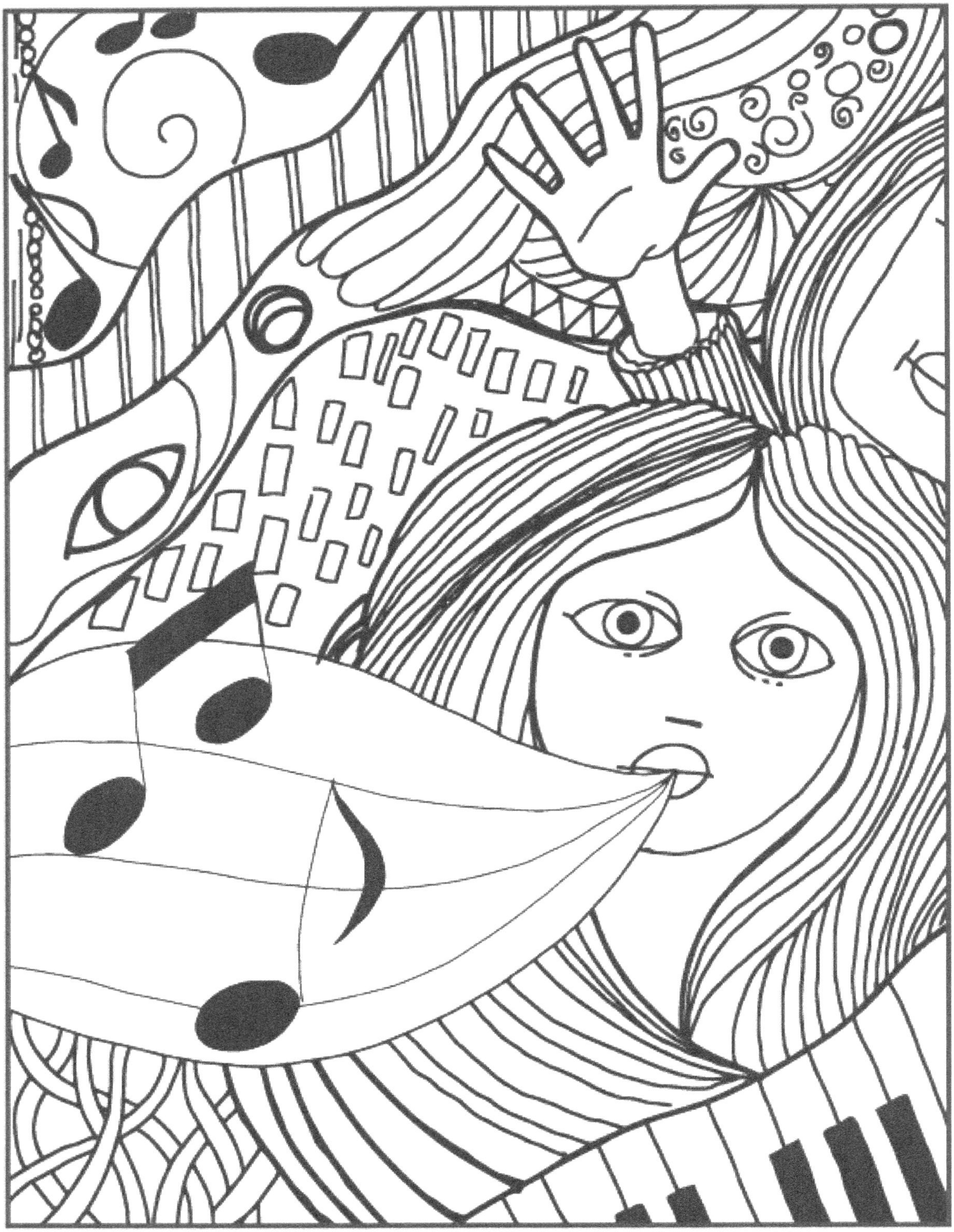

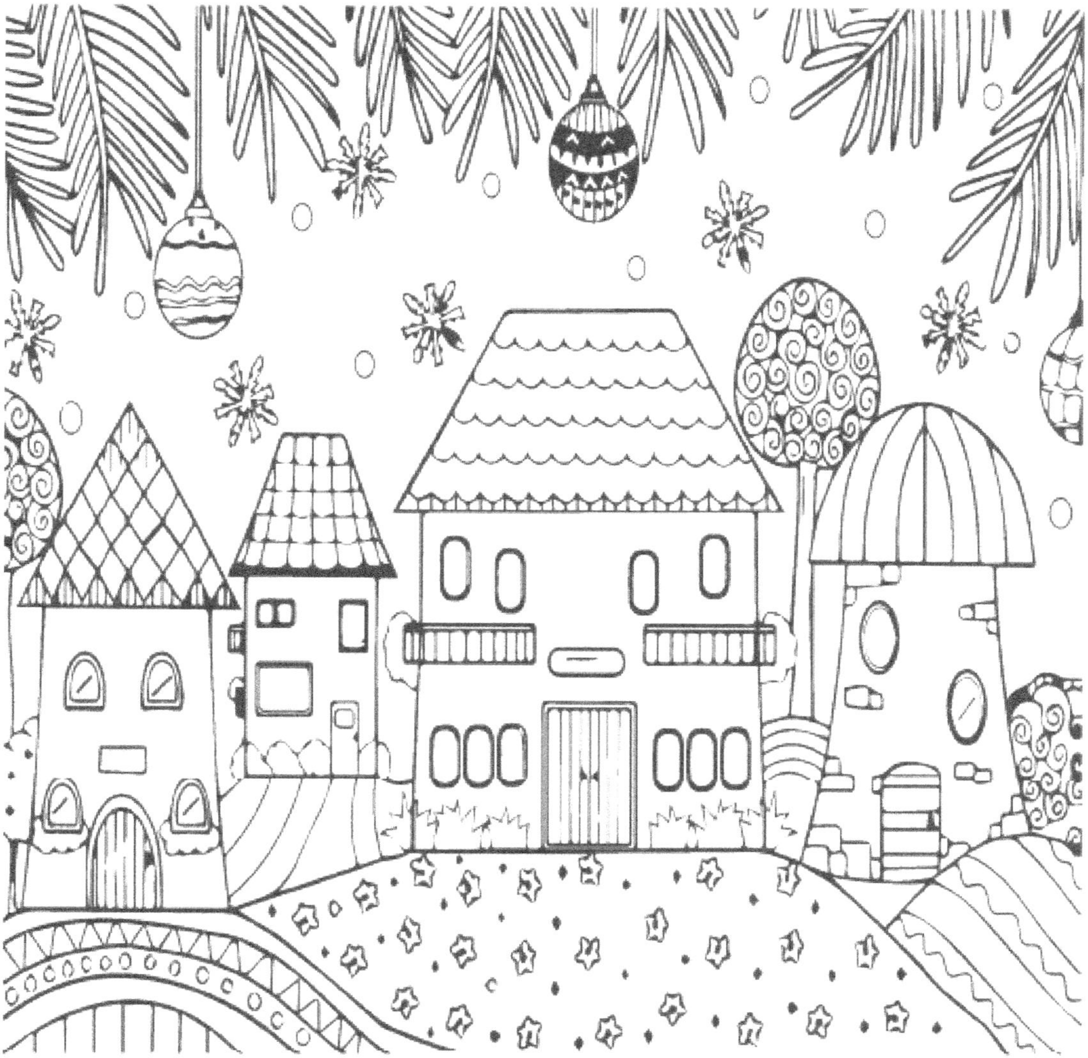

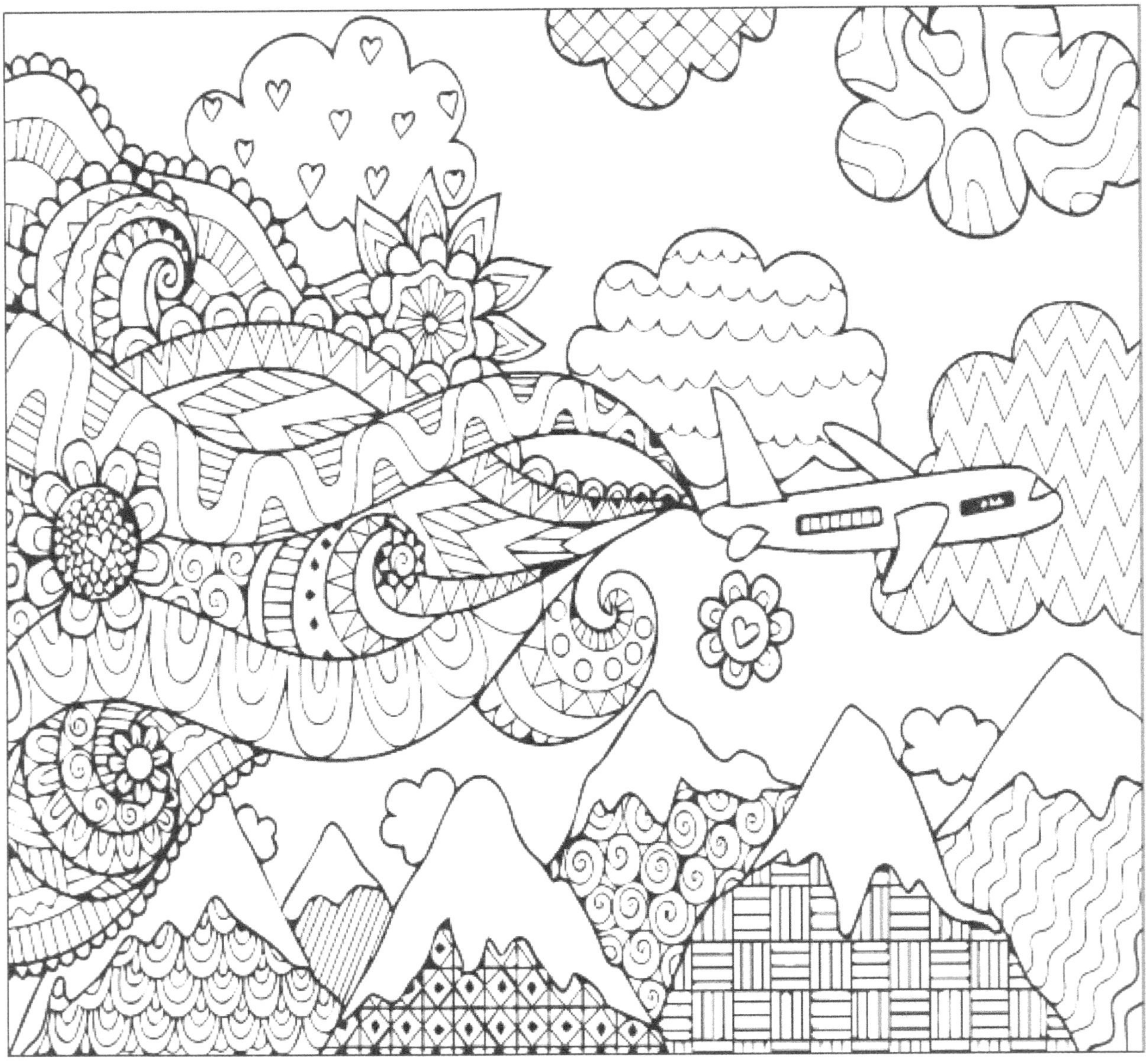

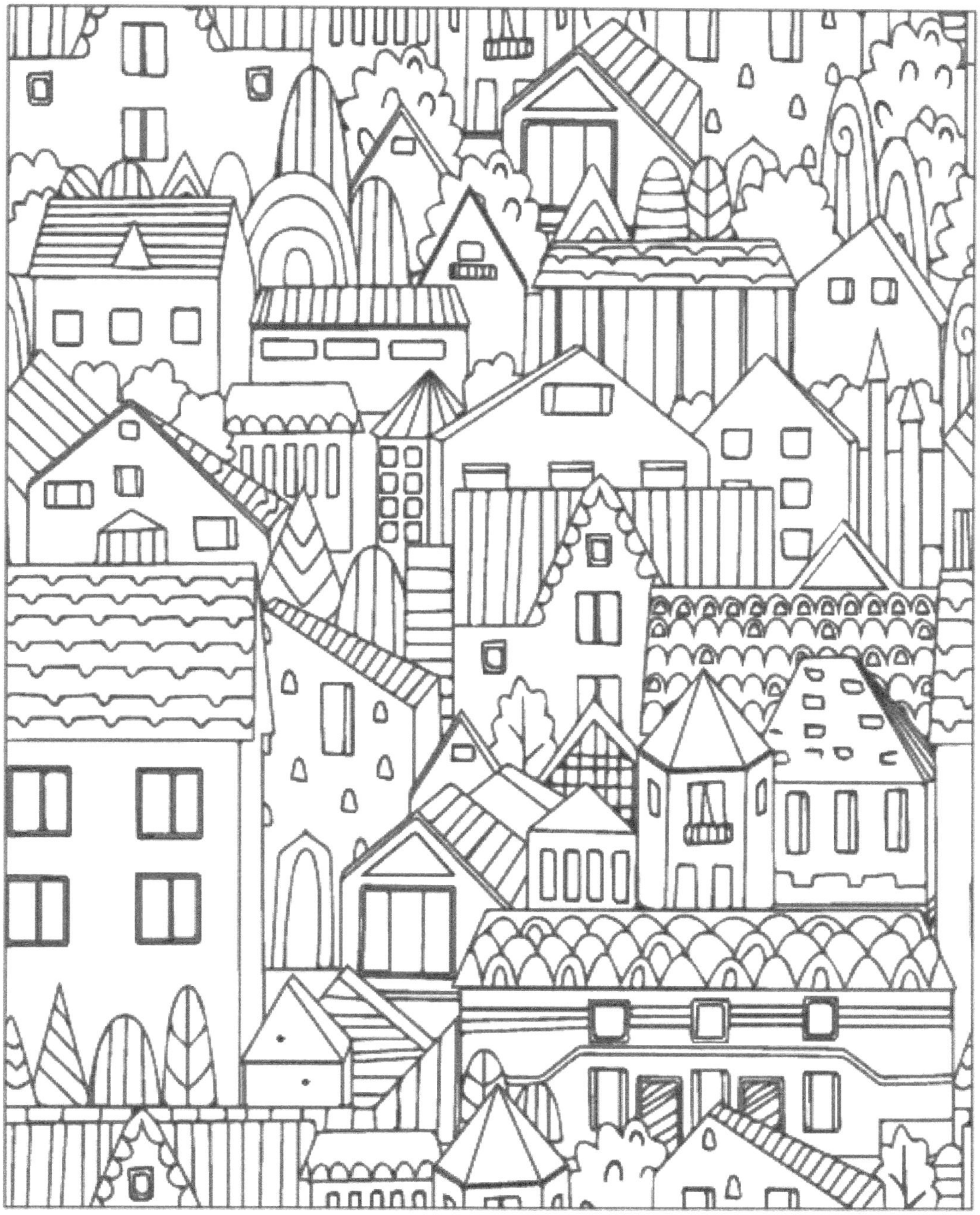

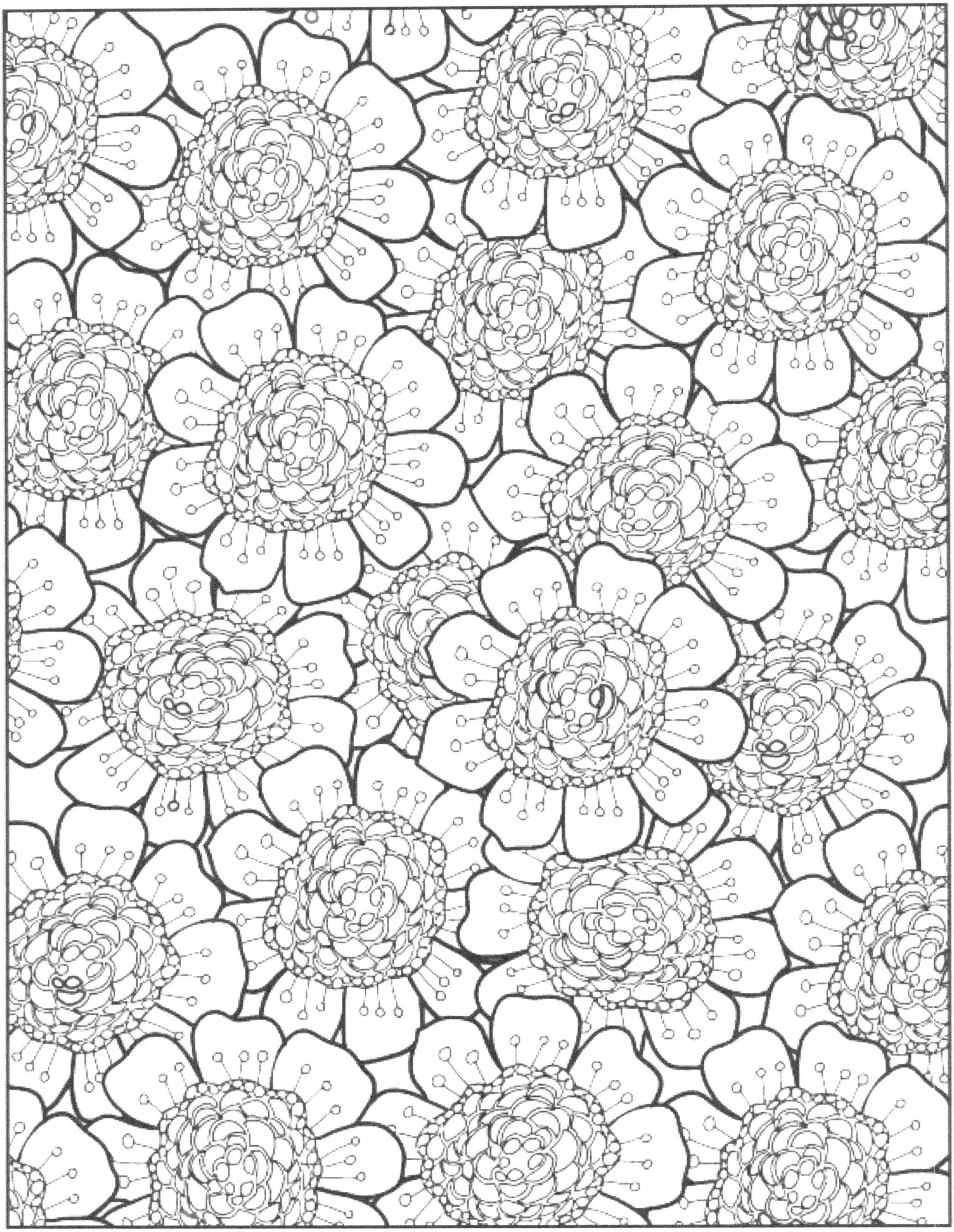

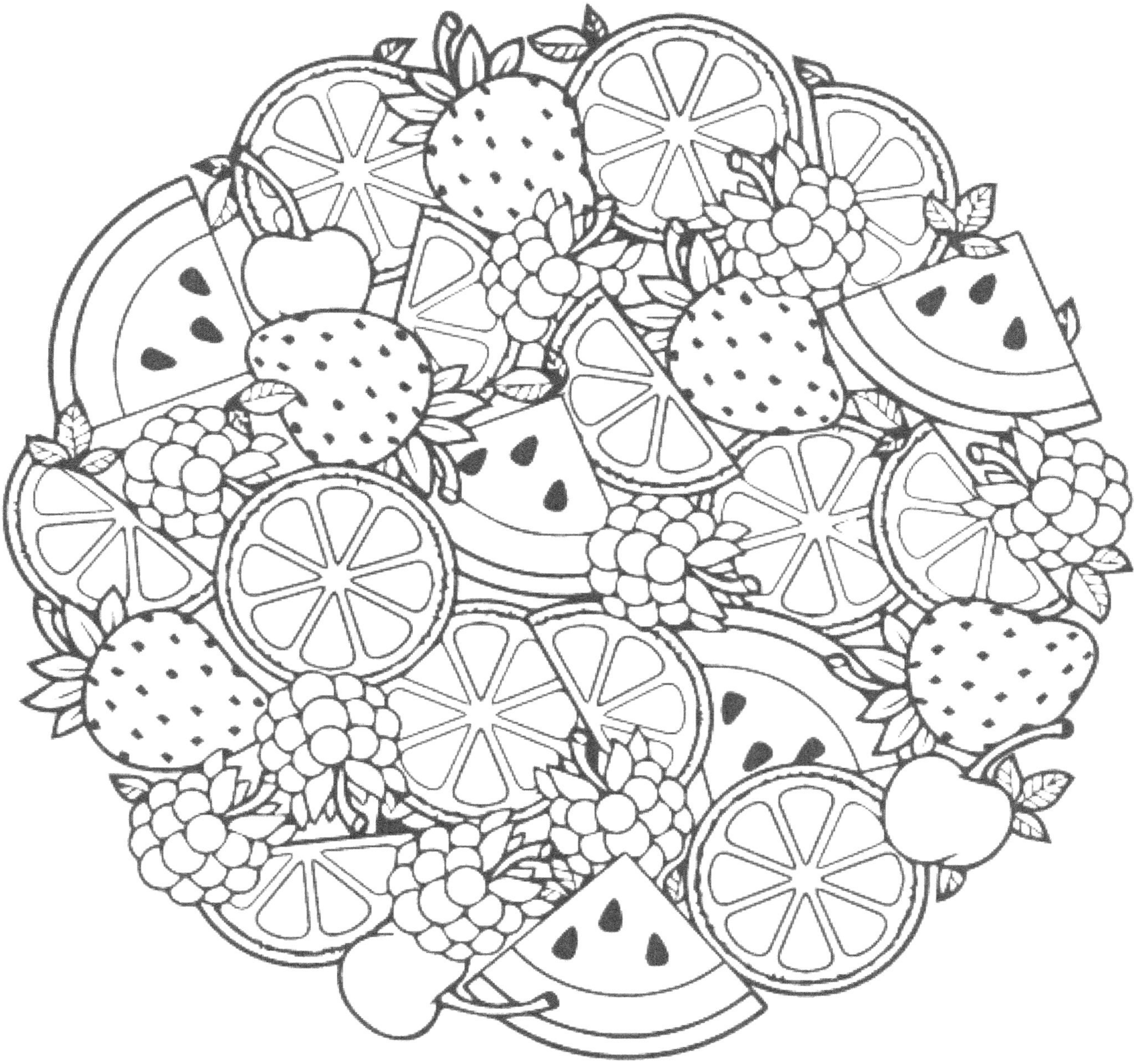

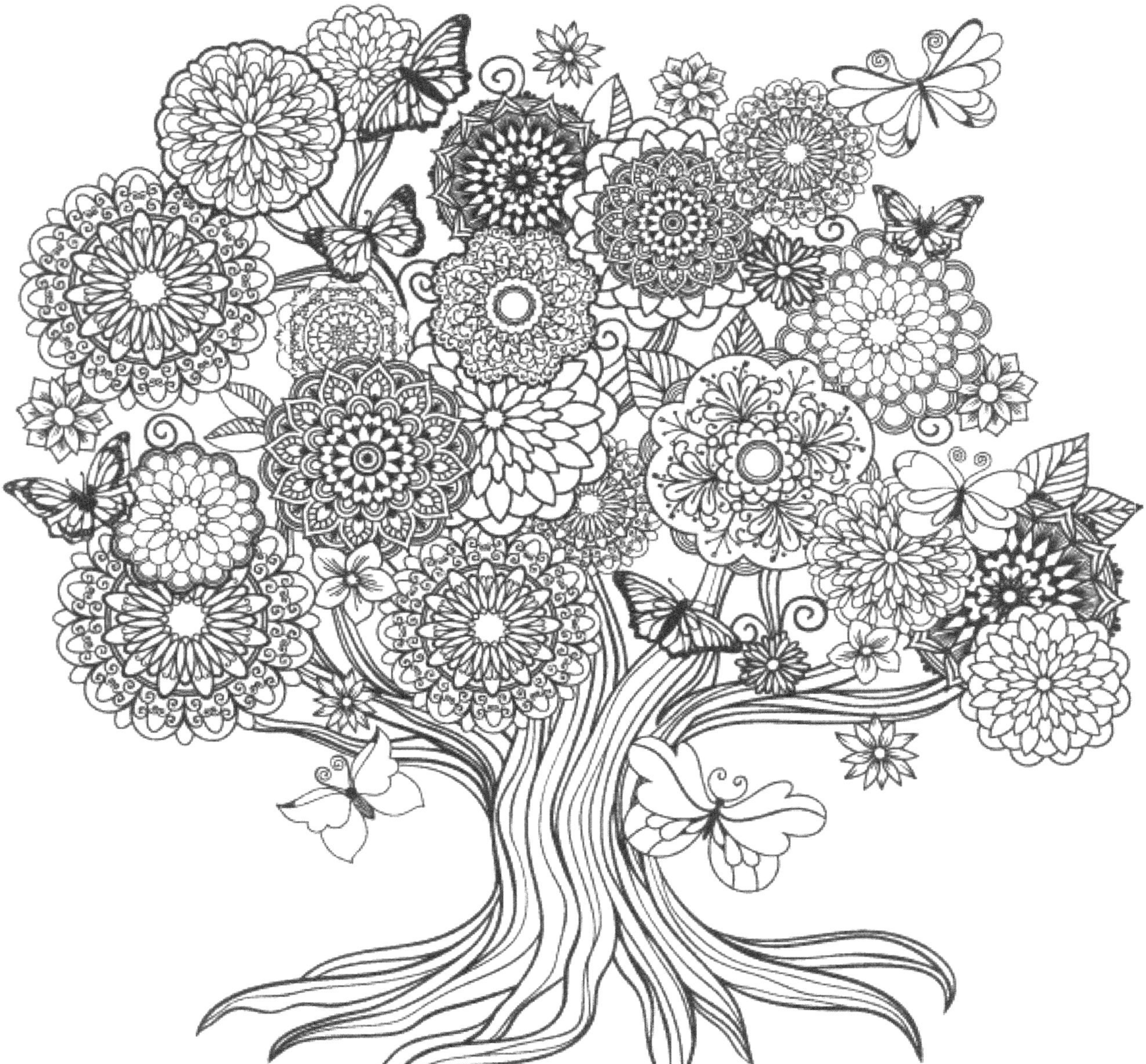

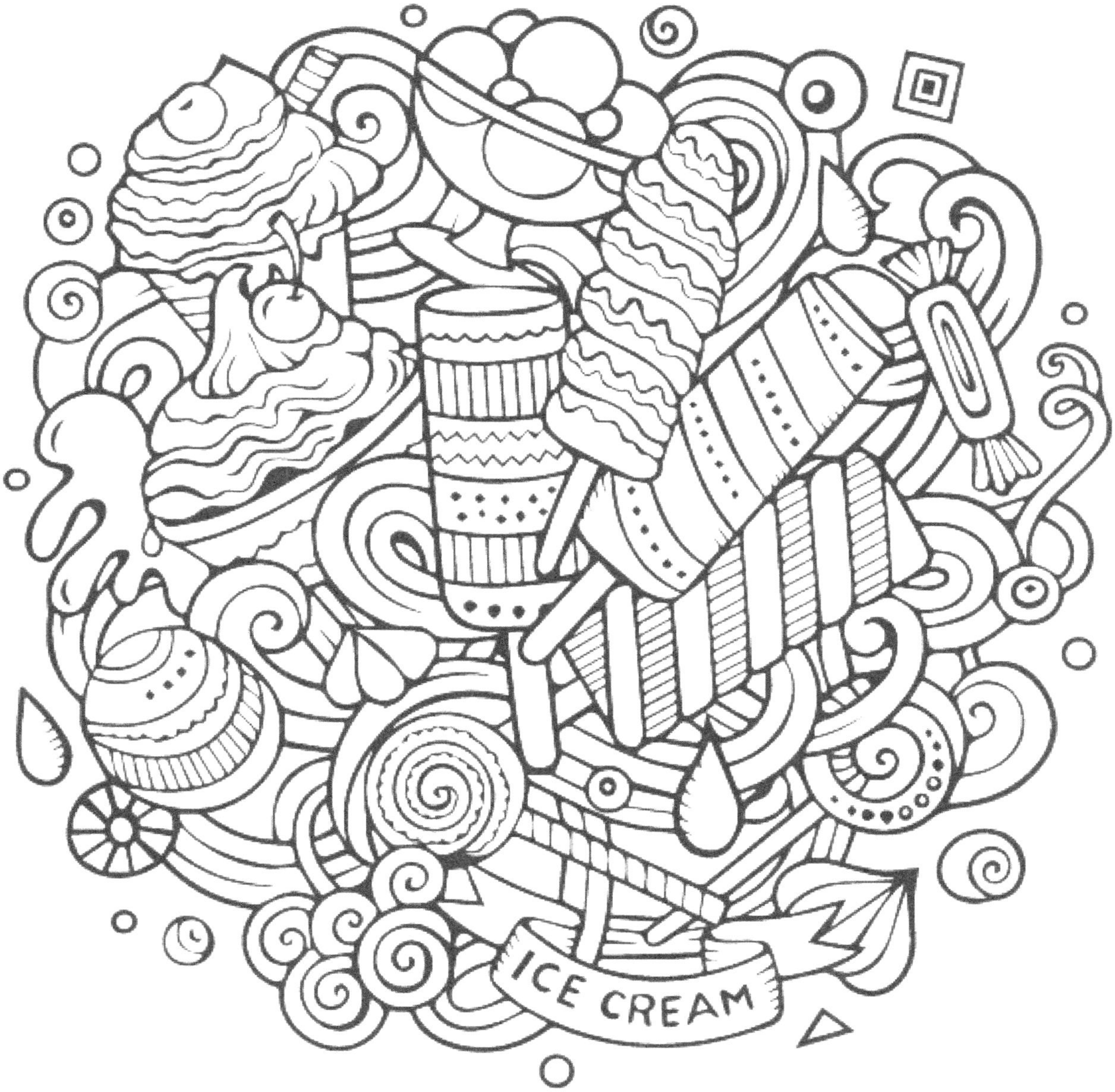
ICE CREAM

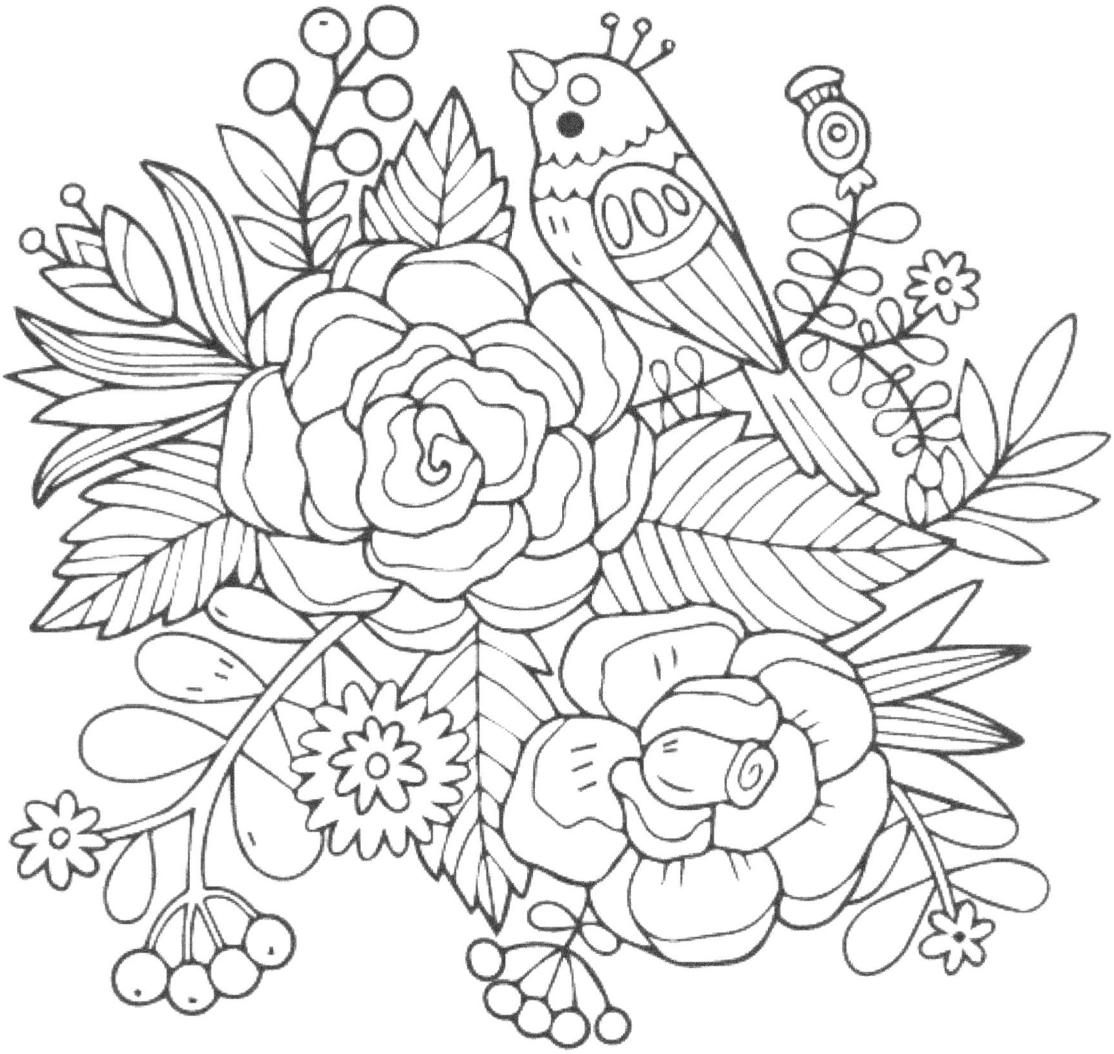

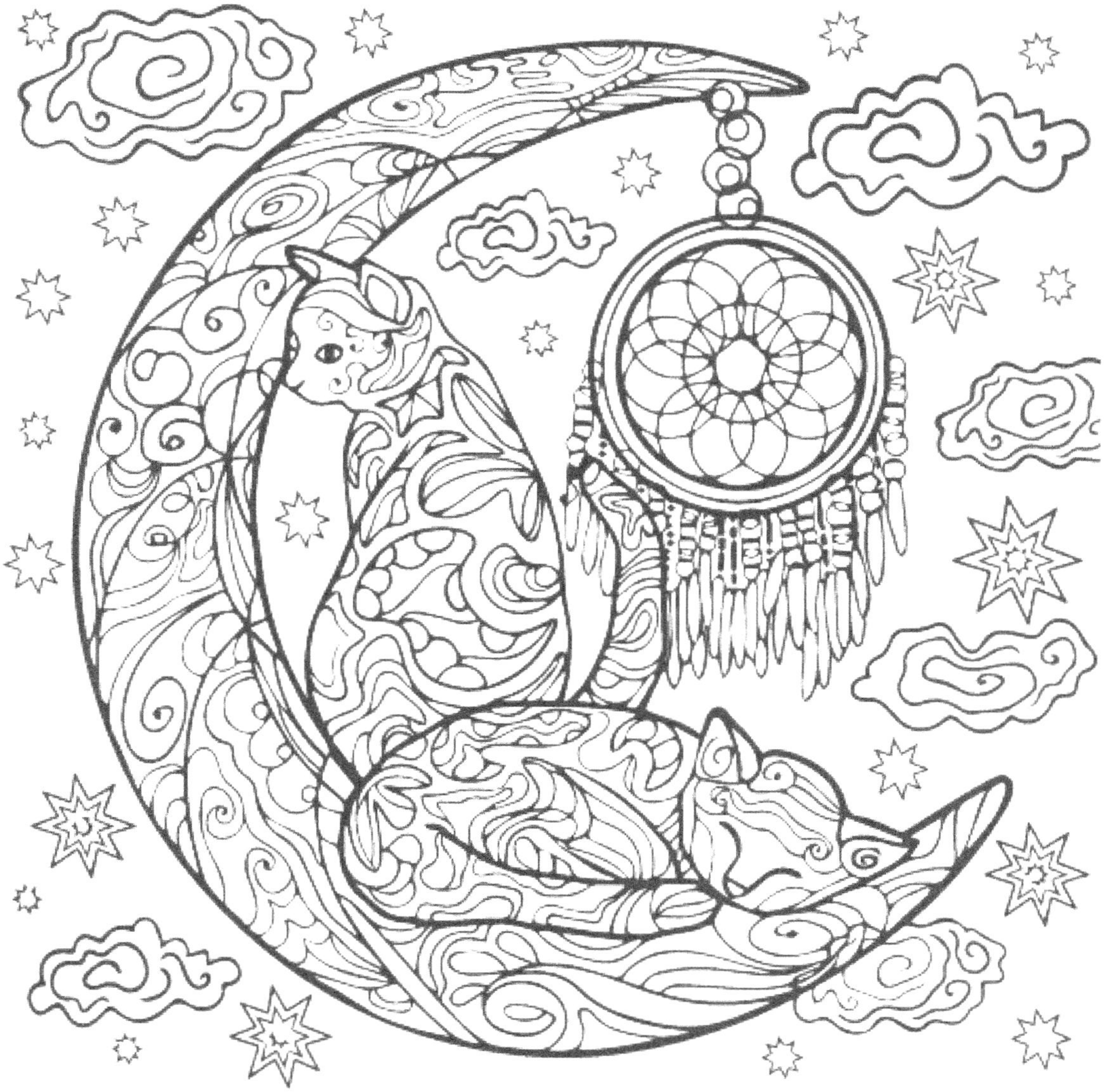

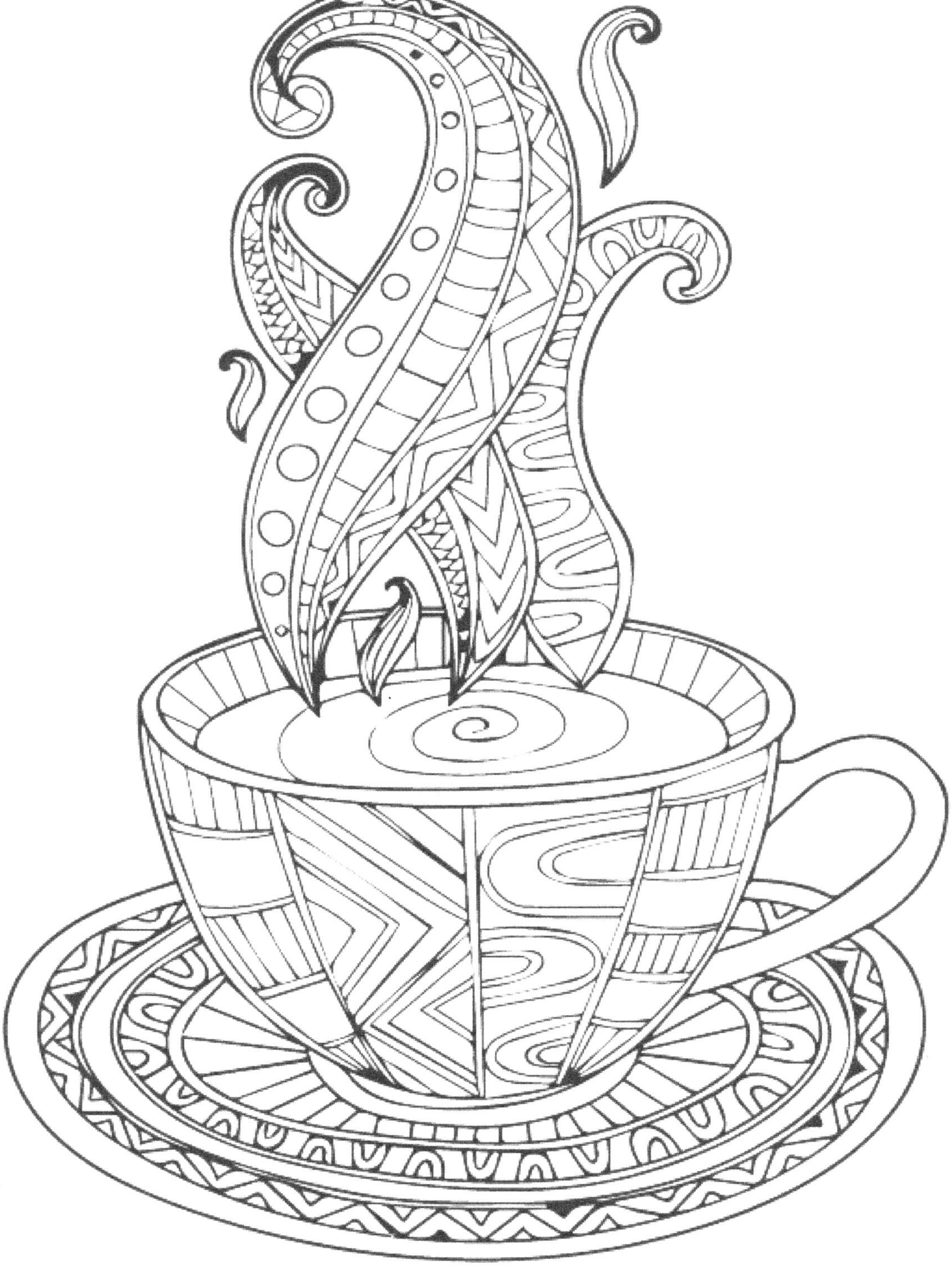

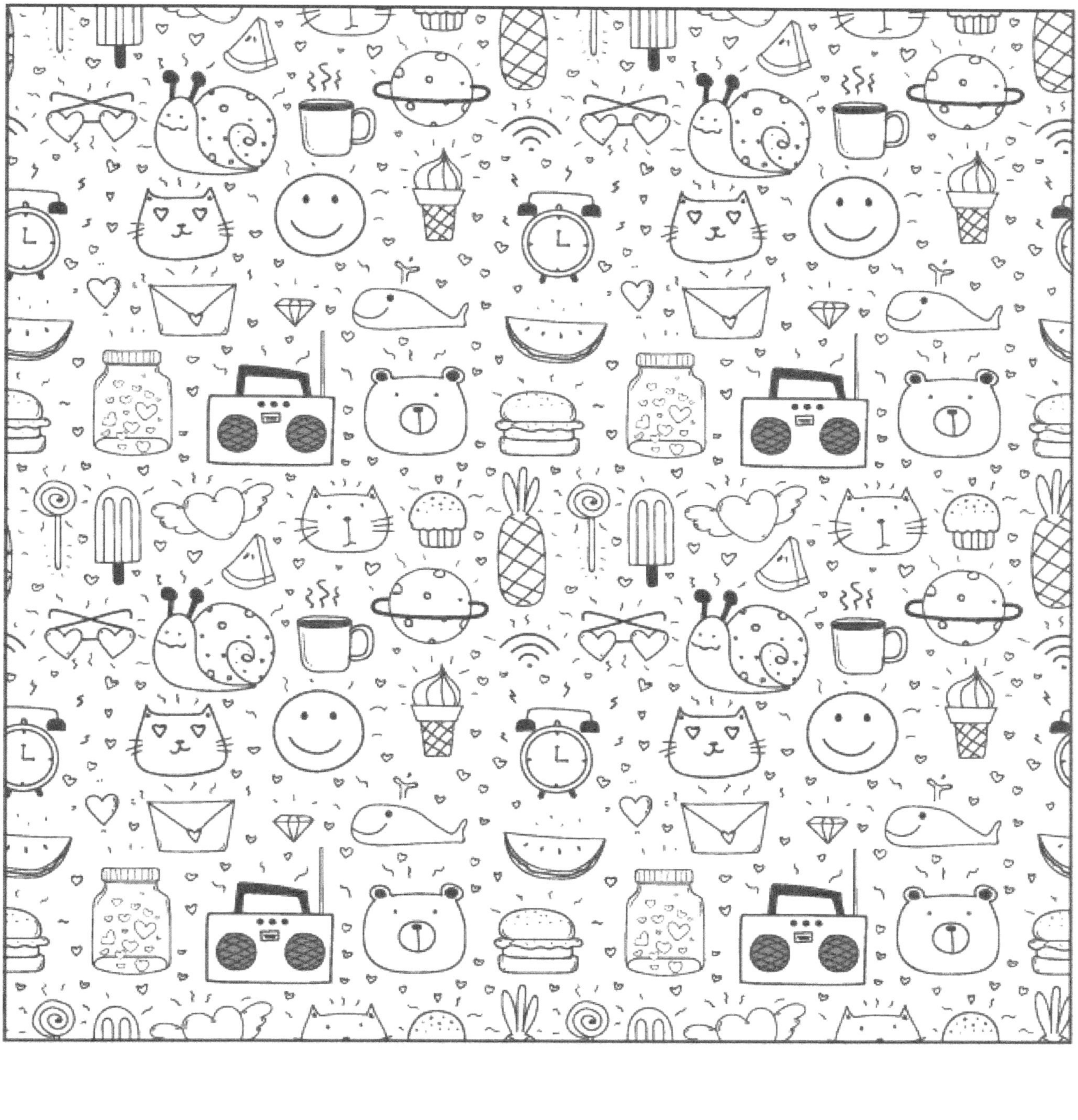

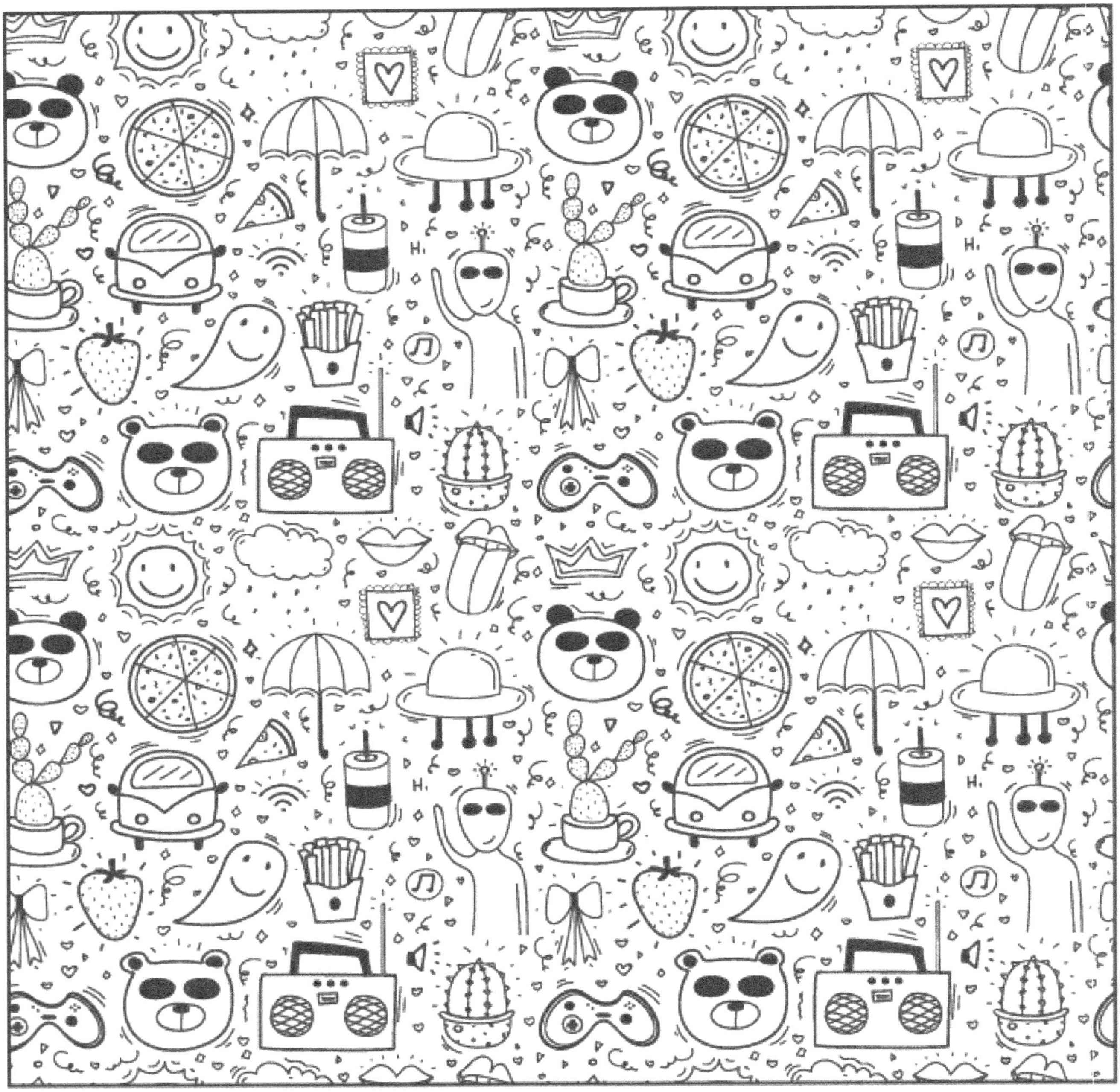

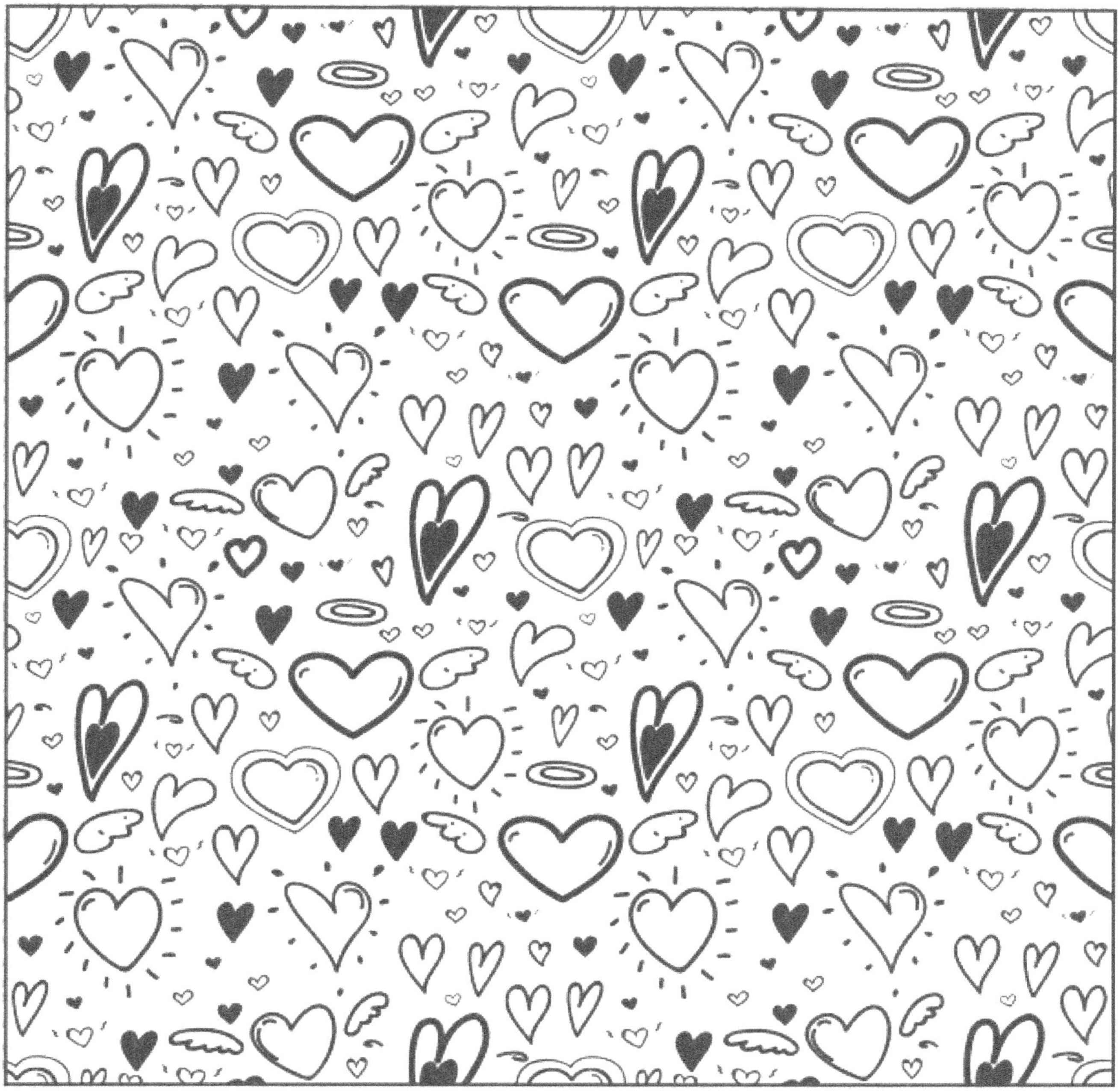

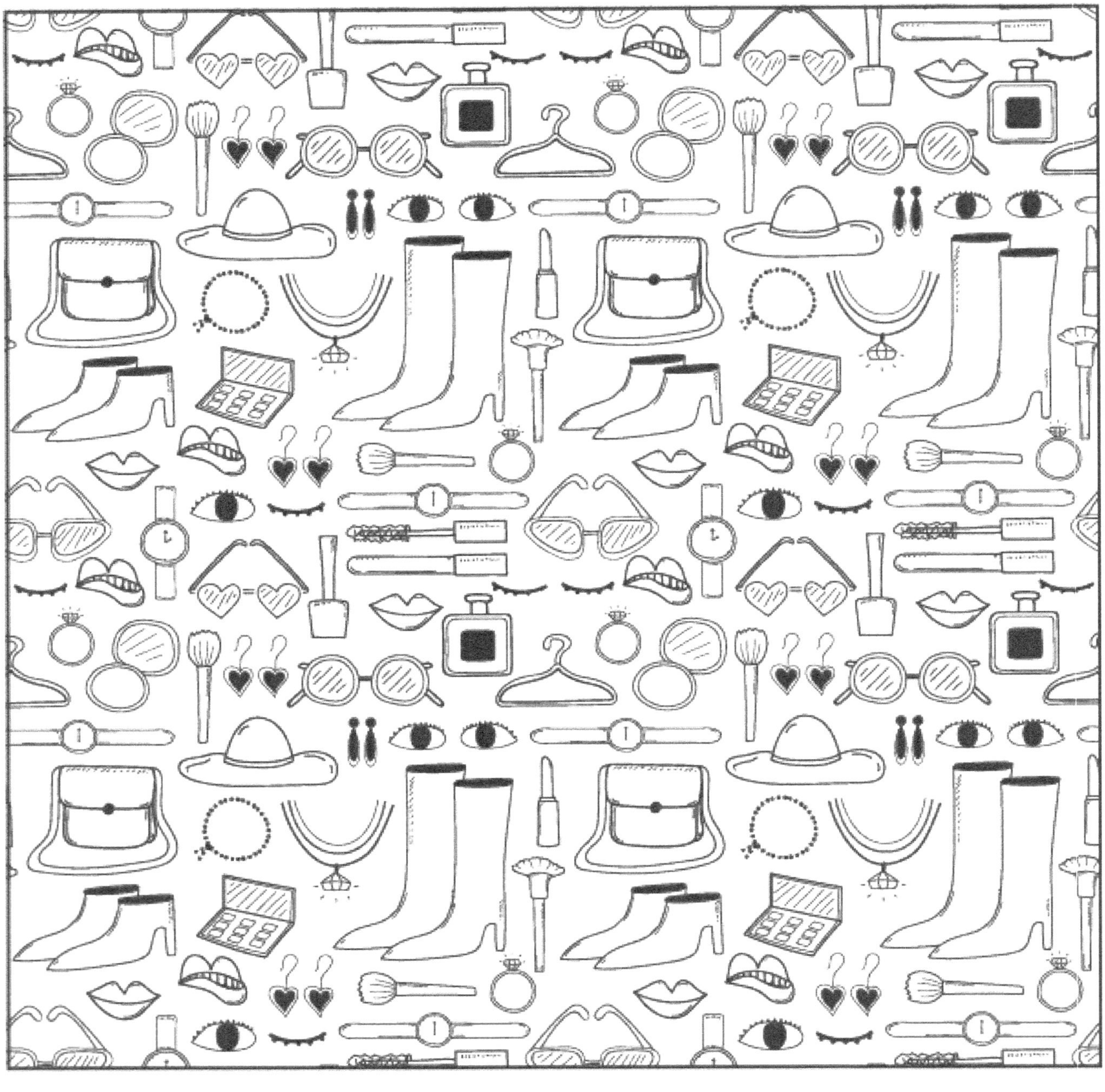

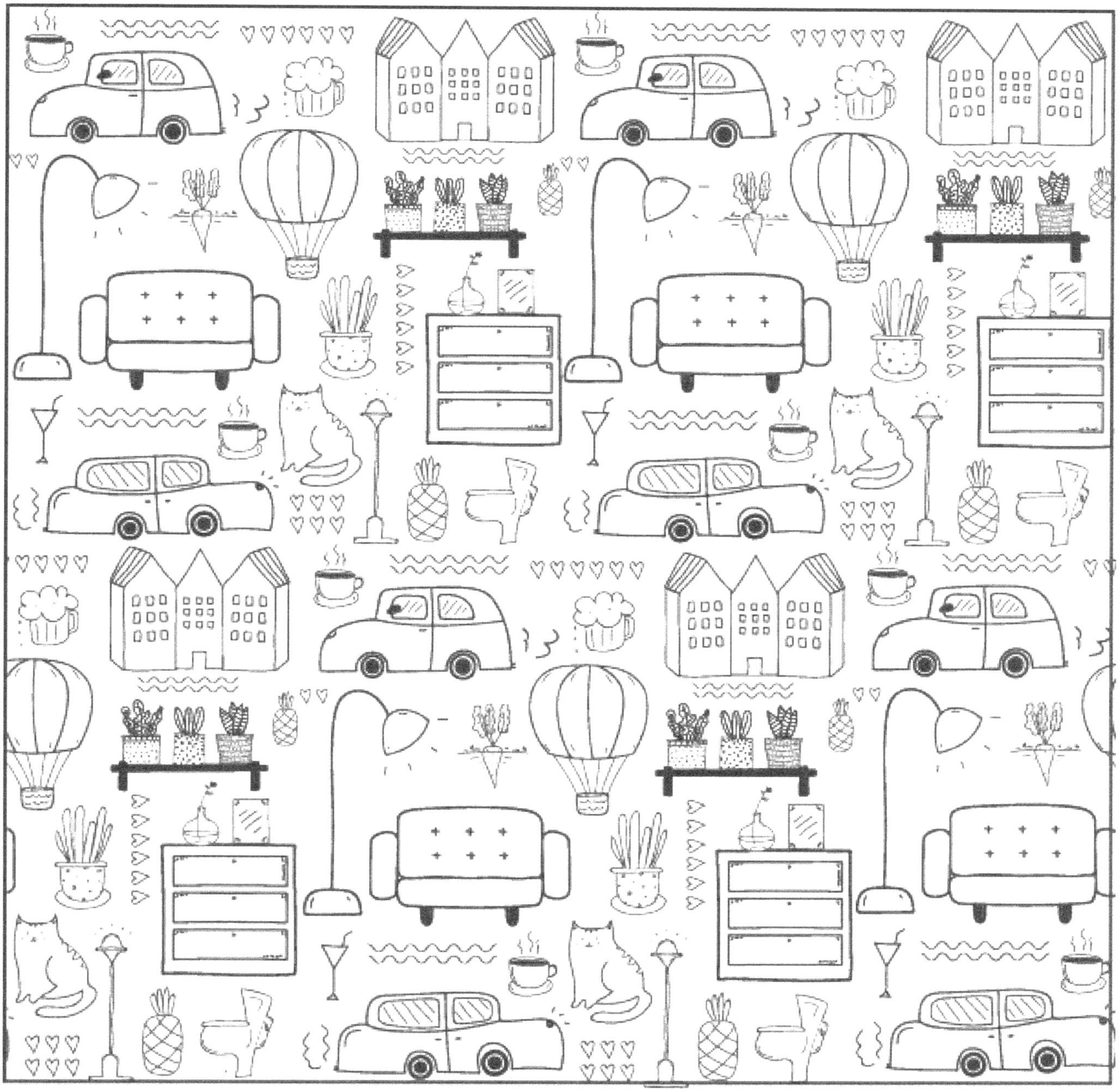

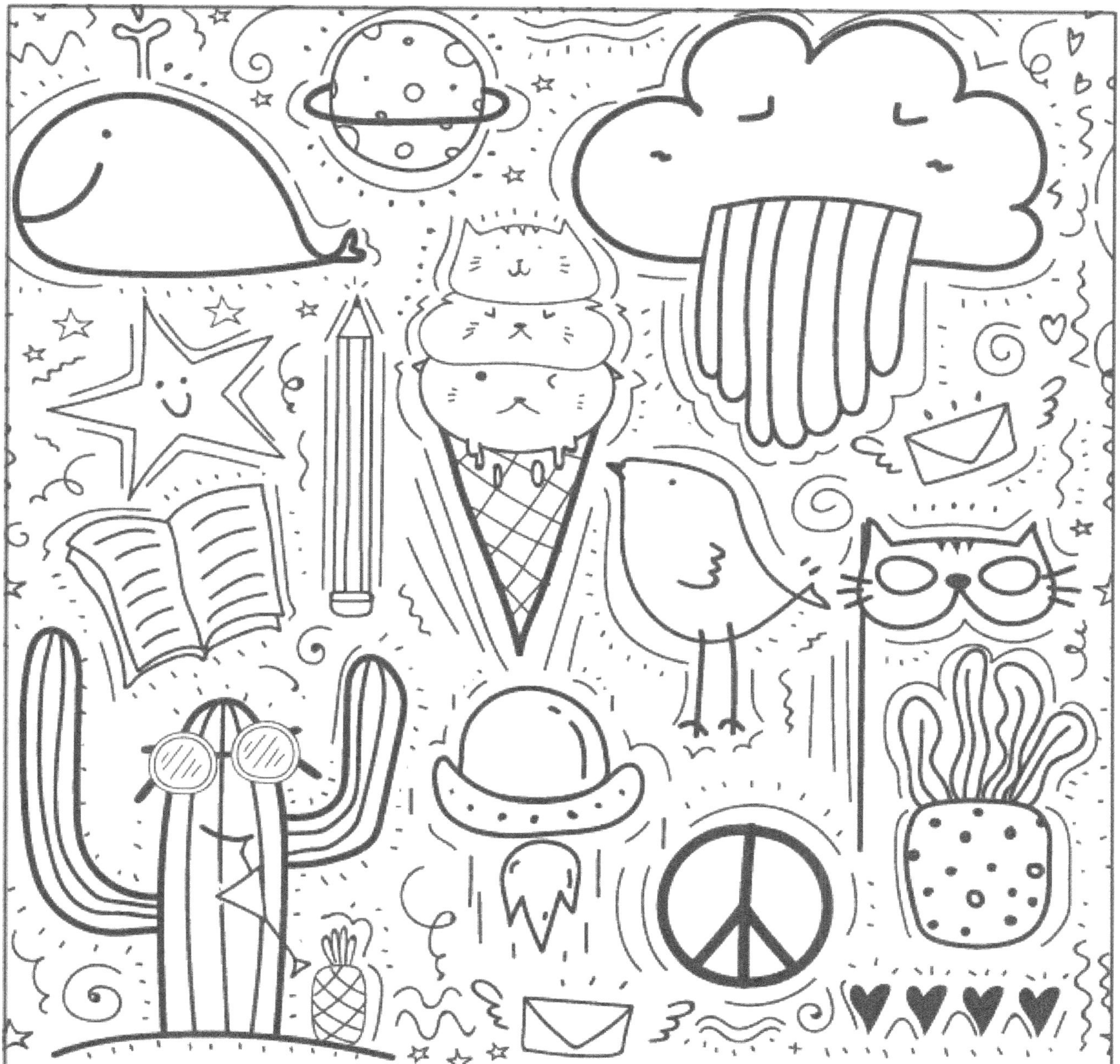

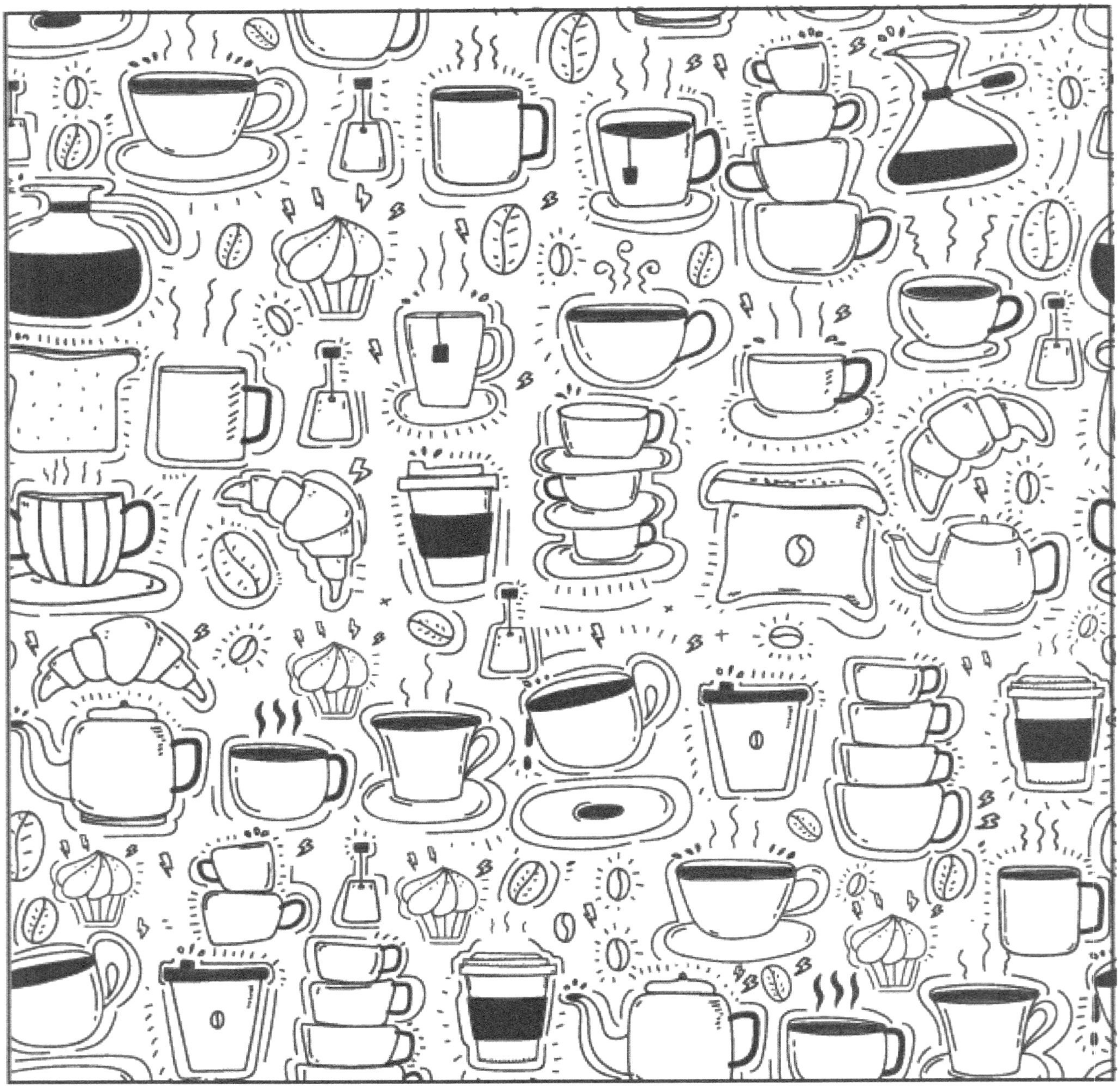

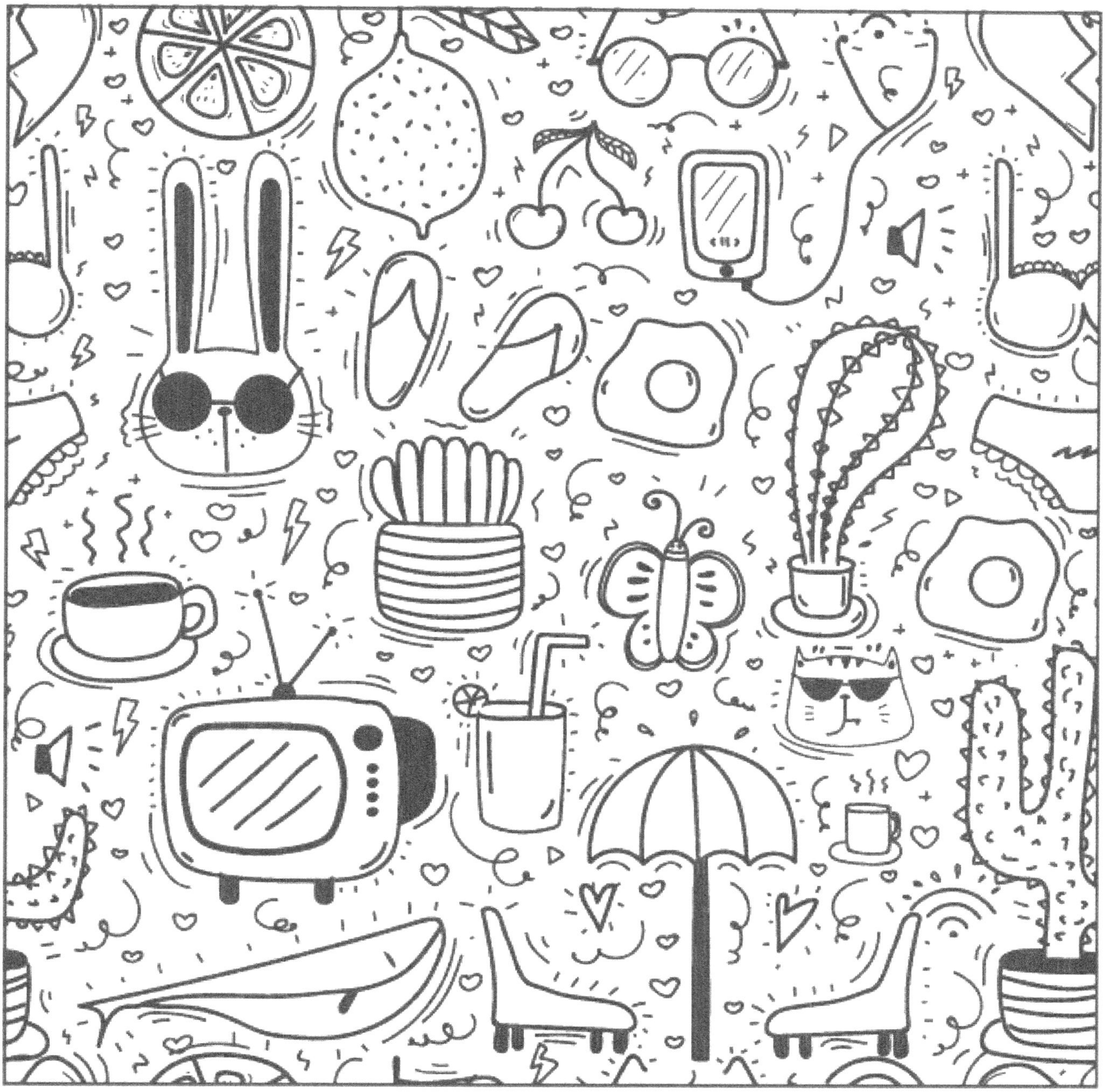

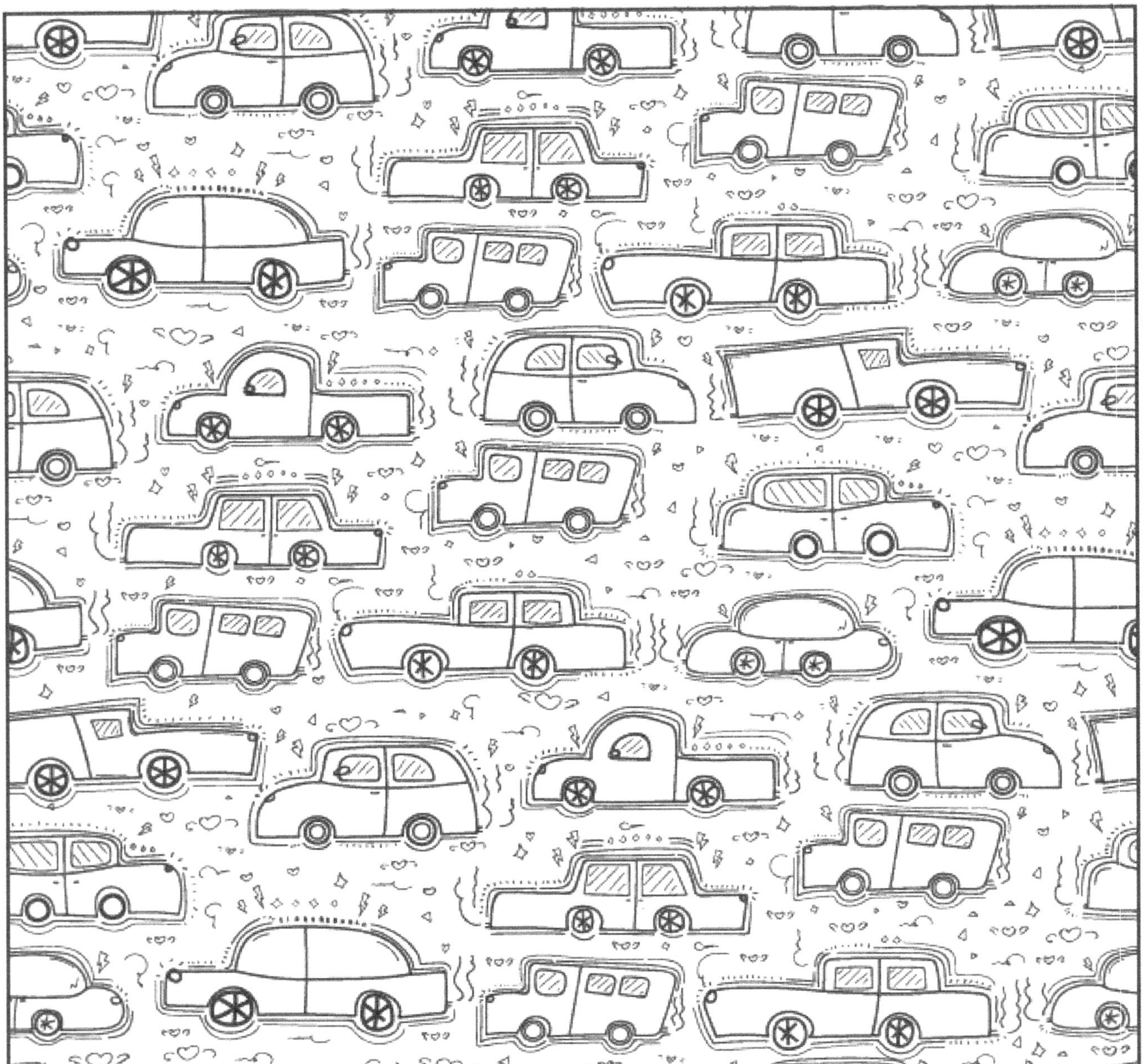

www.ingramcontent.com/pod-product-compliance
Lightning Source LLC
Chambersburg PA
CBHW080952220526
45465CB00008BA/3253
* 9 7 9 8 6 6 3 8 0 4 5 9 2 *